CAMPAIGN 393

THE CIMBRIAN WAR 113–101 BC

The Rise of Caius Marius

NIC FIELDS

ILLUSTRATED BY JOHNNY SHUMATE

Series editor Nikolai Bogdanovic

OSPREY PUBLISHING
Bloomsbury Publishing Plc
Kemp House, Chawley Park, Cumnor Hill, Oxford OX2 9PH, UK
29 Earlsfort Terrace, Dublin 2, Ireland
1385 Broadway, 5th Floor, New York, NY 10018, USA
E-mail: info@ospreypublishing.com
www.ospreypublishing.com

OSPREY is a trademark of Osprey Publishing Ltd

First published in Great Britain in 2023

A catalogue record for this book is available from the British Library.

ISBN: PB 9781472854919; eBook 9781472854940; ePDF 9781472854926;
XML 9781472854933

23 24 25 26 27   10 9 8 7 6 5 4 3 2 1

Maps by Bounford.com
3D BEVs by Paul Kime
Index by Alison Worthington
Typeset by PDQ Digital Media Solutions, Bungay, UK
Printed and bound in India by Replika Press Private Ltd.

Osprey Publishing supports the Woodland Trust, the UK's leading woodland
conservation charity.

To find out more about our authors and books visit
www.ospreypublishing.com. Here you will find extracts, author
interviews, details of forthcoming events and the option to sign up for
our newsletter.

Artist's note

Readers can discover more about the work of illustrator Johnny Shumate at
the below website:

https://johnnyshumate.com

Key to military symbols

Army Group	Army	Corps	Division	Brigade	Regiment	Battalion
Company/Battery	Infantry	Artillery	Cavalry			

Key to unit identification

Unit identifier — Parent unit — Commander

(+) with added elements
(−) less elements

Front cover main illustration: At the battle of Vercellae 101 BC,
the Cimbri commence their ferocious onslaught, their front-rank
warriors fastened together by long chains. The bare-headed Marius
sets a brave example to his men by positioning himself in the
fighting line. (Johnny Shumate)

Title page photograph: A silver *denarius* possibly representing
Marius celebrating his triumph over the northern tribes. (Classical
Numismatic Group, Inc. http://www.cngcoins.com/Wikimedia
Commons/CC-BY-SA-2.5)

CONTENTS

The Roman Empire at the time of the Cimbrian War

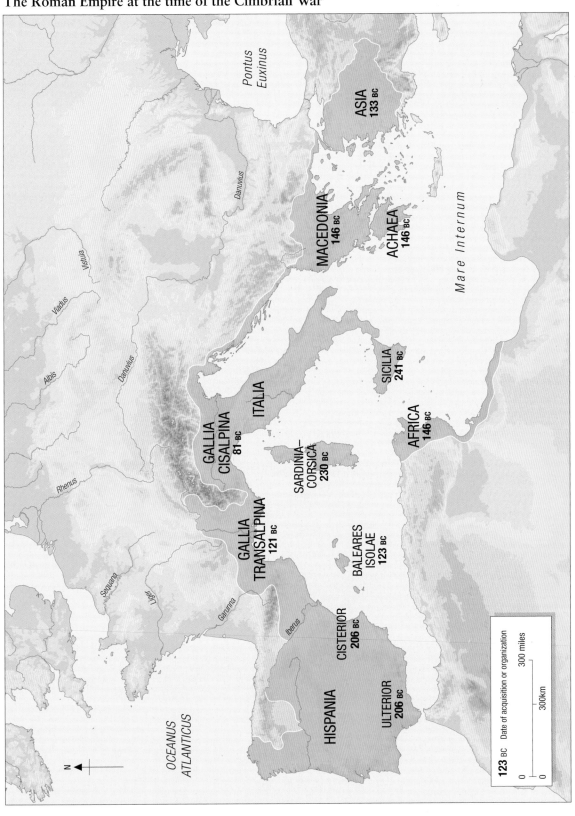

Pontus Euxinus

ASIA
133 BC

MACEDONIA
146 BC

ACHAEA
146 BC

Mare Internum

Danuvius

Vistula

Viadus

Albis

Danuvius

ITALIA

SICILIA
241 BC

GALLIA
CISALPINA
81 BC

SARDINIA–
CORSICA
230 BC

AFRICA
146 BC

Rhenus

GALLIA
TRANSALPINA
121 BC

BALEARES
ISOLAE
123 BC

Sequana

Liger

Garunna

Iberus

CISTERIOR
206 BC

HISPANIA

ULTERIOR
206 BC

*OCEANUS
ATLANTICUS*

N

123 BC Date of acquisition or organization

300 miles

300km

0

0

ORIGINS OF THE WAR

Nations are ultimately built on stories. Perverse as it may seem to us, accustomed as we are to history written by the winners, the Romans had a habit of not forgetting their worst military defeats; they are at least as prominent in Roman historiography and literature as their greatest military victories. Just for the Republic alone we have surviving accounts on the battles of the Allia, the Caudine Forks, the Trebbia, Lake Trasimene, Cannae, and Carrhae, each and every one of them humiliating reverses for Republican Rome. The purpose of Roman historiography was partly to preserve, even to exaggerate, the memory of these battlefield setbacks, so as to hold them up to later generations as cautionary tales. The well-worn watchword that history is written by the victors is far too one-dimensional when it comes to the Romans, and may be even apocryphal in their case. It is in these devastating defeats that they found their most powerful wellspring of moral strength and the will to conquer.

Vegetius, a 4th century AD high-ranking civilian bureaucrat with a sense of history, wrote the *Epitoma rei militaris*. The core of his proposals in his military treatise is a return to the traditional methods of recruitment, training, and deployment that had fully prepared Roman soldiers for the rigours of war. At one point he says the following:

> The Cimbri destroyed the legions of [Quintus Servilius] Caepio and [Cnaeus] Mallius [Maximus] inside Gaul. The remnants were taken up by Caius Marius, who trained them in the knowledge and art of warfare. The result was that they not only destroyed an innumerable host of Cimbri, but of Teutones and Ambrones as well, in a general engagement. But it remains easier to train new men in valour than to reanimate those who have been terrified out of their wits.
>
> Veg. 3.10

Wars sometimes start easily, but it is a tenet of strategy that they are always unpredictable and extremely hard to end. Indeed, once started, they take on a logic of their own. Unquestionably, we can say that of the Cimbrian War (or the Cimbric War, as it is sometimes called). This conflict was to drag on for a dozen years and consumed five consular armies.

CHRONOLOGY

All dates refer to BC.

157   Marius born in Arpinum into a family of *domi nobiles* (i.e. Marii).

138   Birth of Lucius Cornelius Sulla.

133   Marius serves under Publius Cornelius Scipio Aemilianus at Numantia.

129   Marius elected to the military tribunate, perhaps under Marcus Aquillius in Asia.

117   Marius stands for aedileship, but fails.

116   Marius is elected *praetor urbanus* for the following year.

114   Marius is sent to Iberia as *propraetor*.

      First mention of the Cimbri in Graeco-Roman sources.

113   Cnaeus Papirius Carbo is ambushed and defeated at Noreia.

112   Iugurtha takes Cirta (murder of Adherbal) – Rome declares war on Numidia.

      Marius marries Iulia, aunt of Caius Iulius Caesar.

111   Campaign of Lucius Calpurnius Bestia (settlement with Iugurtha).

110   Campaign of Spurius Postumius Albinus.

      Campaign and capitulation of Aulus Postumius Albinus.

109   Marcus Iunius Silanus is defeated and killed by the Cimbri and Tigurini.

      Quintus Caecilius Metellus takes command in Africa (Marius is the senior *legatus*).

      Metellus defeats Iugurtha at the Muthul River, Numidia.

      Unsuccessful siege of Zama.

      The Vaga incident.

108   Romans secure Thala.

      Romans secure Cirta.

      Bocchus allies with Iugurtha.

      Marius returns to Rome in order to stand for the consulship.

107   First consulship of Marius – he enlists the *capite censi* and takes command in Numidia.

      Romans secure Capsa.

      Lucius Cassius Longinus is defeated and killed by the Tigurini.

106   Triumph of Quintus Caecilius Metellus (Numidicus – his granted *cognomen*).

      Battle at the Muluccha fortress.

      Sulla serves Marius as *quaestor* in Numidia.

      Quintus Servilius Caepio takes Tolosa (*aurum Tolosanum* theft).

      Births of Cnaeus Pompeius (Pompey the Great) and Marcus Tullius Cicero.

105   The armies of Cnaeus Mallius Maximus and Caepio are destroyed at Arausio (6 October).

      Betrayal and capture of Iugurtha.

104   Marius' first triumph and second consulship (1 January).

      Marian army 'reforms' introduced.

103   Marius' third consulship.

Construction of the *Fossæ Marianæ* from Arelate (Arles) to the sea.

Mallius and Caepio are condemned and exiled.

101   Marius' fifth consulship.

Defeat of the Cimbri at Vercellae (possibly Vercelli, Italy).

102   Marius' fourth consulship.

Defeat of the Teutones and Ambrones at Aquae Sextiae (Aix-en-Provence).

100   Marius' second triumph and sixth consulship (1 January).

Murder of Lucius Appuleius Saturninus.

Birth of Caius Iulius Caesar.

THE ROMAN CONSULS DURING THE WAR

During their official year, which was named after them, the two consuls held the highest elected political office of the Roman Republic and were irremovable. Originally the consular year had begun on the Ides of March (the month named for Mars, the god of war and agriculture), resulting in the consuls remaining in office for the first few months of the following year, but from 153 BC the beginning of the civil year was altered from 15 March to 1 January. In the list that follows, the Roman numerals in brackets after a name indicate the number of times the man had previously held the consulship, while the abbreviation *cos. suff.* denotes *consul suffectus*, a consul elected to replace another who had either died in office or had resigned before completing his term.

113   Caius Caecilius Metellus Caprarius

Cnaeus Papirius Carbo

112   Marcus Livius Drusus

Lucius Calpurnius Piso Caesoninus

111   Publius Cornelius Scipio Nasica

Lucius Calpurnius Bestia

110   Marcus Minucius Rufus

Spurius Postumius Albinus

109   Quintus Caecilius Metellus (Numidicus)

Marcus Iunius Silanus

108   Servius Sulpicius Galba

Marcus Aurelius Scaurus (*cos. suff.*)

107   Lucius Cassius Longinus

Caius Marius (I)

106   Quintus Servilius Caepio

Caius Atilius Serranus

105   Publius Rutilius Rufus

Cnaeus Mallius Maximus

104   Caius Marius (II)

Caius Flavius Fimbria

103   Caius Marius (III)

Lucius Aurelius Orestes

102   Caius Marius (IIII)

Quintus Lutatius Catulus

101   Caius Marius (V)

Manius Aquillius

100   Caius Marius (VI)

Lucius Valerius Flaccus

COMMAND: CAIUS MARIUS

So-called Marius (Munich, Glyptothek, inv. 319), possibly an Augustan marble copy of a 2nd-century BC original. Caius Marius has often been credited with taking the decisive steps that laid the basis for the professional standing army based on the cohortal legion. By the end of our period of study Rome was the dominant military power in the Mediterranean, and the annual levying of what was in effect a provisional citizen militia was incompatible with the running and maintenance of a world empire. A change would come when, for the levy of 107 BC, Marius opened the army to all citizens regardless of their wealth. (Bibi Saint-Pol/Wikimedia Commons/Public domain)

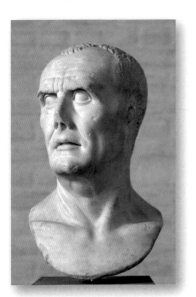

Unhappy the land where heroes are needed.

Bertolt Brecht, *Leben des Galilei* (1939), sc. 13

Caius Marius was born military in character, mind, intelligence, and temperament: much in his later life would confirm it, and his military prowess became a regular *exemplum* in late-antique literature (e.g. Claudian, Eutropius). Marius began his long military career as a cavalry officer, serving with distinction under Publius Cornelius Scipio Aemilianus (*cos.* 147 BC, *cos.* II 134 BC), the greatest Roman of his generation, in the Numantine War (134–132 BC). As Marius was already 23 years old at the time – six years older than the norm for commencing military service – it is feasible that he had already served in Iberia as early as 141 BC, when the consul Quintus Pompeius Aulus conducted a campaign against Numantia and was roundly defeated (Liv. *Per.* 54.1, App. *Iber.* 13.76–8). Plutarch hints as such when he has Marius happy to accept 'the stricter discipline which Scipio was imposing on an army that had lost much of its quality because of expensive habits and a luxurious way of life' (*Mar.* 3.2). Discipline would be another important ingredient of Marius' generalship.

Oddly enough, a young African prince called Iugurtha was serving as the leader of a Numidian contingent under Scipio Aemilianus (Sall. *Iug.* 8.2). The Numidians were horsemen mostly, always the strength of that nation and the same who had done such useful service for Hannibal in the Italian peninsula two generations earlier. Iugurtha was an illegitimate grandson of Masinissa, who, after coming over to Rome's side during the closing stages of the war with Hannibal, had been awarded a kingdom. It was during the siege of Numantia (near modern Burgos, Castilla y León, Spain) that Iugurtha had earned Scipio Aemilianus' approval by his martial qualities, but it also encouraged a Roman belief that their most dangerous opponents were men whom they themselves had taught how to fight (Vell. 2.9.5). In any case, the two young cavalry commanders were probably well acquainted and, like the Numidian prince, Marius was to enhance his reputation outside Numantia when he 'encountered and laid low an enemy in sight of his general' (Plut. *Mar.* 3.3, cf. Val. Max. 8.15.7). For a man of relatively humble origins, it must have looked as if the future belonged to him – unless his rivals devoured him first.

In many ways, the spectacular career of Marius was to provide a model for the great warlords of the last decades of the Roman

Republic. He came from the local aristocracy (*domi nobiles*) of the central Italian hill-town of Arpinum (Arpino), which had received Roman citizenship only 31 years before his birth. In 107 BC, just shy of his 50th birthday, Marius became consul, which proved to be the first of seven consulships, more than any man had held before. It was not simply the number that was unprecedented, but the nature, for five were to be held in consecutive years between 104 BC and 100 BC, whilst the seventh he was to seize in 86 BC, as he had taken Rome itself with armed force. He was to die, in his early 70s, only 17 days after entering office (Plut. *Mar.* 46.5; cf. Diod. 37.29.4, *Vir. ill.* 67.6), leaving behind him a crisis that was to spiral into civil war. Marius' spectre was to haunt the Republic for decades to come.

NEW MAN

One of the bonds that held Roman society together was the relationship between client (*cliens*) and patron (*patronus*). This relationship came in a wide variety of forms and guises, but all were based on the mutual exchange of favours and benefits. Roman society was thus vertically structured in terms of obligation-relationships, called clientele (*clientela*). At its crudest, a *patronus* offered protection to his clients (*clientes*), who attended him and offered support and services in return. As the *cliens* of a privileged man might himself be the *patronus* of still less-important men, *clientelae* could be mobilized as effective voting-machines. It takes little effort, therefore, for us to appreciate how much the *patronus–cliens* relationship could affect the workings of the Roman state. If a *patronus* was elected to political office, his *clientela* could look forward to gaining some lucrative state contracts.

Panoramic view of Arpino, Lazio, as seen from what was originally the Samnite acropolis. Arpinum, as it was then called, produced two consuls of the late Roman Republic, Caius Marius and Marcus Tullius Cicero, both *homines novi* (they were also distant relatives). Arpinum had been a community of Roman citizens since 188 BC (Liv. 38.36.7, Fest. 262 L), after having enjoyed a favourable legal status vis-à-vis Rome (viz. *civitas sine suffragio*, 'citizenship without voting rights') for more than a century. Marius was part of a second generation of Roman citizens in his hometown: a community that, while being integrated with Rome, remained a *municipium* with its own self-governing bodies. Instead of seeking public office locally, Marius chose an altogether different and more difficult route. (Piergiorgio Mariniello/Wikimedia Commons/CC-BY-SA-3.0)

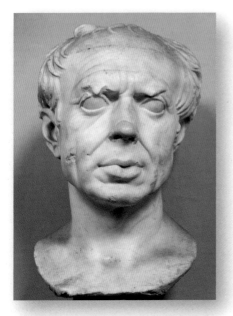

So-called Marius (Vaticani, Museo Chiaramonti, inv. 1488), marble bust dated to 1st century BC. Caius Marius held an unprecedented series of consulships during the last decade of the 2nd century BC, and defeated Iugurtha of Numidia and later the much more serious threat to the Italian peninsula from migrating Cimbri and Teutones. Marius managed to contain the situation in the north, and in two successful battles – the first at Aquae Sextiae in Gallia Transalpina (102 BC) and the second at Vercellae in Gallia Cisalpina (101 BC) – the Teutones (and their allies, the Ambrones) and the Cimbri were successively beaten. With the Cimbrian War over, his loyal camp of supporters proclaimed Marius the third founder of Rome, and its saviour. (Marie-Lan Nguyen/Wikimedia Commons/CC-BY-SA-3.0)

The Romans saw nothing wrong or corrupt in a politician handing out state contracts to his *clientes*. It was simply how their political system worked.

Marius belonged to the *clientela* of the Caecilii Metelli, one of the most powerful and influential families (*gentes*) in Rome at this time. Indeed, this was the age of the Caecilii Metelli, who had held a remarkable sequence of 12 consulships, censorships, or triumphs in as many years (Vell. 2.11.3), though some, most notably Scipio Aemilianus, called them stupid (Cic. *Orat.* 2.267). Having clawed past the patrician Scipiones, who had held this position since the war with Hannibal, the Caecilii Metelli had 'prevailed by their mass and by their numbers. Their sons became consuls by prerogative or inevitable destiny; their daughters were planted out in dynastic marriages' (Syme 1956: 20). It had been in 123 BC, when Marius became *quaestor* (Val. Max. 6.9.14, cf. *Vir. ill.* 67.1), that this powerful family had taken a keen interest in his career, and so it was the Caecilii Metelli who helped him to gain a plebeian tribunate in 119 BC, when he was 38 years old (Plut. *Mar.* 4.1, cf. Val. Max. 6.9.14 whose work generally emphasises the peaks and troughs of a politician's career).

Marius soon demonstrated that he was no flunky, successfully passing a *plebiscitum*, the *lex Maria*, which allowed for the narrowing of the *pons* (gangway) across which each voter passed to fill in and deposit his ballot tablet (Cic. *Att.* 1.14.5, *Leg.* 3.17.38, *RRC* no. 292/1, cf. Plut. *Mar.* 4.2–3). To vote in the *comitia* a man mounted one of several bridges and walked along it to a platform, where he dropped his vote in an urn (*cista*). And yet, of course, the voters were viewed by everyone – in particular the senatorial aristocrats – and Marius was troubled by the likelihood of undue pressure and harassment.

True to form, it was his patrons the Caecilii Metelli who blocked Marius' election to the aedileship (Plut. *Mar.* 5.1) – an office mainly concerned with public life at street level – two years later. The family intervened again when he stood for *praetor urbanus* for 115 BC, but this time they were unable to keep him out. Marius scraped in with the lowest number of votes possible, and as a consequence there were allegations of electoral bribery (*ambitus*; Val. Max. 6.9.14). In essence, bribery represented a form of patronage, a liberating force for the Roman voters, which could now market its voices. Whether this was a politically motivated prosecution, or one of merit, Marius prevailed at the trial, but by the thinnest of margins. The number of votes for his guilt and innocence were dead equal, and he had to be given the benefit of the doubt (Plut. *Mar.* 5.5).

In 114 BC, Marius went to Iberia as *propraetor*, which was fortunate as it was a region about which he would have acquired some knowledge. As governor of Hispania Ulterior he proved his competence, campaigning successfully against bandits while adding to his personal fortune by establishing the Iberian silver mines on a sound footing. On returning to Rome at the end of 113 BC, he married Iulia (Plut. *Mar.* 6.3–4). This was a real political coup, as the Iulii Caesares were a patrician family of undoubted antiquity and prestige – though far from affluent or prominent in this age (they last held the consulship in 157 BC, the year of Marius' birth). Marius,

for his part, not only brought his personal fortune but also his attachment to the *populares* cause in politics, something that was to prove of great benefit to his wife's nephew, Iulius Caesar, in future decades.

THE AMBITIOUS SOLDIER

At a very early stage of his political career, Marius had shown himself to be an independent man, and highly popular for his challenges to the *nobiles*. In particular, Marius delivered a vigorous attack on a broad front against their corruption, exclusiveness, and incapacity in a speech Sallust (*B Iug*. 85.4–40, cf. Plut. *Mar*. 9.2–4) puts in his mouth – a splendid piece of polished Latin. Ruffling the people's spirit to dissent, Marius was not one to interest himself in doing what had always been done. Nevertheless, it would be his reputation as a soldier that would make his name, and it was the war against the Numidian king Iugurtha, begun in 112 BC, that would give him his first real opportunity to stand out, and eventually become the best war leader the Roman army had at the time.

Marius went to the kingdom of Numidia in 109 BC as one of the legates under his *patronus*, the consul Quintus Caecilius Metellus, apparently tasked with the command of the cavalry. Clearly, Marius had set himself right with the epoch-making house of the Caecilii Metelli, who were on the whole intransigent *optimates* (i.e. supporters of the 'best' men), in the years following his provocative programme as a tribune of the plebs.

Les Trémaïé (*Les trois Maries* in Provençal), Baux-de-Provence, *département* of Bouches-du-Rhône, rock carved bas-relief depicting three Romans, two females and one male. The French archaeologist Isidore Gilles postulated that two of the figures represented Caius Marius (left) and his wife Iulia (right), who was the aunt of Iulius Caesar. The central figure he believed to be Martha, a Syrian prophetess who Marius 'carried around with him in great state' (Plut. *Mar*. 17.1, cf. Frontin. 1.11.12). Marius appears to have been obsessed with his own personal destiny. Sallust (*B Iug*. 63.1–2) tells us that he was encouraged in his ambition to be a consul (for the first time) by a prophetess at Utica who prophesied that he would have a most distinguished career. (Carole Raddato/Wikimedia Commons/CC-BY-SA-2.0)

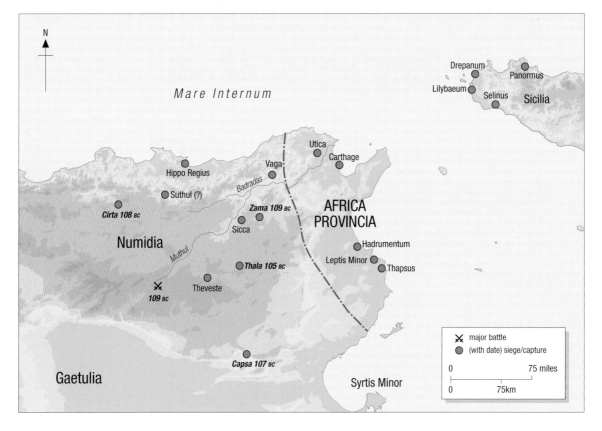

It must be understood that the social gulf between the Caecilii Metelli and a man of Marius' background was great, and must have been obvious to all their contemporaries.

The political geography of North Africa at this time was essentially quadripartite. In 146 BC, following the destruction of Carthage by Scipio Aemilianus, Rome had annexed Carthaginian territories, creating the province of Africa (*Africa provincia*, roughly coextensive to eastern and central Tunisia). This left to the Numidian king, Micipsa, much of the land his father, Masinissa, had appropriated from the Carthaginians, as well as his own kingdom (western Tunisia and eastern Algeria). To the west, in Mauretania (western Algeria and northern Morocco), was found the kingdom of Bocchus, the future father-in-law of Iugurtha. In a long band of land along the pre-desert lived the Gaetuli, a group of tribes who lay outside the two kingdoms of Numidia and Mauretania and who resisted any attempts to tax or control them. In 118 BC, Micipsa bequeathed his kingdom to his two legitimate sons, Hiempsal and Adherbal, and, going on an earlier recommendation of Scipio Aemilianus, to the illegitimate son of his younger brother, Iugurtha, whom the king adopted. The kingdom was thus entrusted to the rule of the three of them.

Ambitious and unscrupulous, Iugurtha was to put to death first one then the other of his adoptive brothers, and made himself master of Numidia. A senatorial commission, headed by a disreputable gentleman by the name of

Lucius Opimius (*cos.* 121 BC), had been sent to settle Numidian affairs after the murder of Hiempsal. The Roman historian Sallust, who was keen to illustrate the moral decline of Rome, implies the delegation fell under the spell of Iugurtha and thus prudently recommended the kingdom be divided between him and Adherbal. Apparently, Iugurtha had learnt while serving in Iberia the venality of many of the Roman *nobiles* ('*omnia Romae venalia*', Sall. *B Iug.* 20.1, cf. 8.1).

Notwithstanding this settlement, four years later Iugurtha captured and sacked Adherbal's royal capital, the hill-top fortress of Cirta (Constantine, Algeria). After he had treacherously murdered both his last remaining rival and the resident Italian traders (*negotiatores Italici*) who had shared the defence of Cirta, the Senate as a matter of course decided on war. In spite, according to Sallust, of Iugurtha's lavish use of bribery, the senators were bent on punishing the Numidian king, and after two unsuccessful campaigns (111–110 BC) dispatched the quixotic but able Metellus against him (Sall. *B Iug.* 43.1). To serve as his *legati*, the consul took with him Rutilius, a special favourite of the Caecilii Metelli, and Marius (ibid. 46.7, Vell. 2.1.1, Plut. *Mar.* 7.1, *Vir. ill.* 67.1).

On his arrival in the province of Africa, Metellus found an army rotten and decayed. The soldiers had abandoned military routine to spend weeks in ill-disciplined idleness, not bothering to fortify or lay out their camp as per army regulations, and shifting it only when forced to by lack of locally available forage or because the stench of their own waste became unbearable. Soldiers and camp followers plundered at will. This was the shambolic army Metellus assumed command of in 109 BC, just as spring slid into summer (Sall. *B Iug.* 44.1–5).

Metellus' response was a traditional one, namely to put the men back under the tight, all-embracing discipline that the Roman army was famed for. Traders, sutlers, and other unscrupulous parasites were expelled, and soldiers forbidden to buy food – many had been in the habit of selling their rations of grain to purchase ready baked civilian bread rather than eating the coarse camp bread they had to prepare and cook themselves, which was often a recipe for gastronomic disaster. Ordinary ranks were barred from keeping their own servants or pack animals. Metellus ordered gruelling daily drills to reintroduce the men swiftly to the intricacies of military life, as well as to improve battle skill and physical endurance. From now on, the army broke camp every morning, and marched fully equipped to a new position, where it constructed a marching camp as if in hostile territory. 'By these methods he was able to prevent breaches of discipline, and without having to inflict many punishments he soon restored the army's morale' (Sall. *B Iug.* 45.6).

Having knocked the army into fighting shape, Metellus went on to win a hard-fought battle beside the Muthul River (Wäd Mellag), but found it impossible to bring the Numidian king to heel. Finally holed up in the Atlas Mons (Tell Atlas), Iugurtha would only skirmish with the Roman forces or fight them on his own terms. Though military incompetence was partly to blame, Sallust, one of the late Republic's most pungent observers of

Stèle du Chevalier Libou (Algiers, Musée national des antiquités), a pre-Roman stele from Abizar, Algeria, depicting a bearded Numidian horseman. The stele is dated around the period when the headstrong Iugurtha of Numidia waged an insurgent war against Rome. He is armed with three javelins and carries a small round shield. Riding without either bridle or saddlecloth almost from infancy, Numidians rode small, swift horses that appeared scrawny but were capable of enduring where heavier, stall-fed mounts could not. Numidian horsemen were excellent in hit-and-run and pursuit. In war Numidian tribal troops followed their own chieftains. Such forces could be raised quickly, but also melted away at sowing or harvesting time. The best warriors were horsemen – especially those from the arid steppe areas of the Sahara, where the nomadic life still prevailed – though the bulk of Numidian armies were composed of lightly armed foot warriors. (Meriam Cherif/Wikimedia Commons/ CC-BY-SA-4.0)

domestic polarization and decline, sees the constant failure to overcome Iugurtha as primarily down to the corruption of the senatorial aristocracy. On the one hand, as Sallust admits, Metellus proved to be a competent opponent whom Iugurtha could not bribe. On the other hand, however, Sallust portrays the twisty, slippery Iugurtha both as the 'noble savage', immune to the corruption of Roman civilization, and as the 'ignoble barbarian', a paradigm of that hoary chestnut, 'Punic' perfidy.

WAR WITH IUGURTHA

For our particular story, one of the most important aspects of the war with Iugurtha was the extraordinary rise of Marius. Despite two successive campaigns, Metellus had failed to bring the war to a swift conclusion. The problem was that Iugurtha was still at large in the empty land. Metellus, for that reason, resorted to corrupting Iugurtha's confidant Bomilcar (the plan very nearly succeeded), coupled with a draconian policy of reducing the urban communities in Numidia so as to deprive the king logistically. Marius was to employ the same strategy against Iugurtha, so we should be wary of any criticism of Metellus' conduct in this war.

Trionfo di Mario (New York, Metropolitan Museum of Art, inv. 65.183.1), oil on canvas (1725–29) by Giovanni Battista Tiepolo (1696–1770). Painted to decorate the *salone* of the Ca' Dolfin, Rio di Ca' Foscari, Venice, the Latin inscription on the banderol reads: 'The Roman people saw Iugurtha led in triumph loaded with chains', a line from the historian Florus (1.36.17). Iugurtha is shown ahead of Marius, the main attraction of the latter's triumph held on 1 January 104 BC. Plutarch (*Mar.* 12.6) states that the booty carried in the triumphal procession amounted to 3,007lb of gold, 5,775lb of silver bullion, and 287,000 *drachmae*. It was Marius' first moment of glory. Incidentally, Tiepolo found a place for himself among the bystanders on the left edge: he is turning his head to stare at us. (Metropolitan Museum of Art/ Wikimedia Commons/CC0 1.0)

Sallust (*B Iug.* 66.3–4, 67.3) records the massacre of the Roman garrison at Vaga (Béja, Tunisia), with the exception of its commander Titus Turpilius Silanus, after the town's betrayal to Iugurtha. Metellus retook Vaga within two days, and he promptly put its inhabitants to the sword (ibid. 69.3). Turpilius himself was arrested, tried before Metellus' *consilium*, convicted of treason, and executed after a scourging. Sallust (ibid. 69.4) claims Turpilius was *civis ex Latio* (a Roman citizen of Latin origin), and for that reason could not be executed without a formal trial. Yet, it appears that Turpilius was only a first-generation Roman citizen, which allowed Metellus to conveniently ignore his legal status and treat him as a non-Roman, and a treacherous one at that. It so happens that Turpilius, as well as serving as Metellus' *praefectus fabrum*, was also a guest friend (*hospes*) of his, and Marius was to use this tragic episode against Metellus in his campaign for the consulship. According to Plutarch, however, it was Marius who had argued for the death penalty, which Metellus was forced to accept. When it was discovered that the charge was false, Marius then claimed that the miscarriage of justice had been the sole fault of Metellus (Plut. *Mar.* 8.1–2).

Surprisingly, Sallust makes no reference to this incident, but does describe how Metellus, when Marius sought permission to return to Rome to seek the consulship, exhibited the characteristic haughty arrogance of the proud, dyed-in-the-wool Roman *nobilitas*. Sallust, who, after all, had been a partisan of Caesar before turning his hand to penmanship, suggests that Metellus was absolutely mortified that a man of Marius' background and social standing could even think of such a thing. Whatever his exact view of the matter, he flatly denied Marius' request. Sallust continues the story:

> When Marius kept on renewing his petition, [Metellus] is alleged to have told him not to be in such a hurry to be off. 'It will be time enough', he added, 'for you to stand for the consulship in the same year as my son.'
>
> Sall. *B Iug.* 64.4

The *nobilis* general's response was certainly spiteful, as his son was a young man only in his early 20s and currently serving on his father's *consilium*. In other words, Marius could canvass for the consulship when he was a septuagenarian. Marius could hardly have taken the jibe with equanimity.

Respect for the unwritten rules of belonging to a *clientela* dependent on a *patronus* meant one had to accompany him, go to his house, and include oneself publicly in the circle of his friends and *cliens* in order to secure backing and assistance from him. Marius, realizing he had no support from his *patronus*, started to seek elsewhere. To this end, he exploited the prevailing political atmosphere in Rome, thereupon making contacts of his own, particularly among the equestrians engaged in business in Africa, those *negotiatores* whose activities had been drastically curtailed by the Numidian war, and building up his own military reputation by claiming that he would quickly finish off Iugurtha (Vell. 2.11.2).

Though elected on the equestrian and popular vote, Marius is best seen as an opportunist and not as a *popularis*, that is to say, an aristocrat who, proving untrue to his own background, was a genuine reformer. Sallust (*B Iug.* 65.5) reckons that everything favoured the election of Marius as consul, and essentially Marius was exploiting popular feeling with regards to the apparent lack of swift action against Iugurtha – the war had dragged and the expected Roman victory was not forthcoming – and so should not be regarded as 'anti-senatorial'. For four years, Iugurtha had defied the might of Rome, and many leading senators were believed to have accepted his bribes, and at least a couple of the generals who had conducted the first campaigns against him were suspected of treason. In any event, they had been incompetent.

Even so, Metellus' partisans in the Senate did not designate Numidia-Africa as a consular province, so ensuing his continuing command there as a proconsul (Sall. *B Iug.* 62.10). It was a reasonable step on the Senate's part; the plodding but honest Metellus had done much better than his incompetent predecessors, even if his progress was slower than the people had hoped for. Besides, Metellus was familiar with the enemy and the army (one now hardened to campaigning in the semi-arid wastes of Numidia under his steady command). All in all, he was the best choice to finish off the war and restore some of the old senatorial lustre.

However, it was not to be, thanks to some chicanery on Marius' behalf by Titus Manlius Mancinus, who, as tribune of the plebs, went before the *populus Romanus* and called upon them to decide who was to take charge of the ongoing war in Numidia. By the unprecedented move of a *plebiscitum* passed by the *concilium plebis*, Marius duly received what he desired, Numidia-Africa as his consular province. Though there was no clear

So-called Sulla (Munich, Glyptothek, inv. 309), possibly an Augustan marble copy of an earlier prominent Roman from the 2nd century BC. Lucius Cornelius Sulla (138–78 BC) hailed from a distinguished patrician family, though his grandfather was the last to hold public office, serving as a *praetor* in 186 BC. A courteous character of cold, calculating cruelty with a reputation for devious clairvoyance and a wicked memory, this blood-soaked dictator-to-be would ruthlessly crush all those who he believed had stood in his way or had risen up against him. Marius was to come at odds with Sulla, their bitter quarrel provoking the first of Rome's civil wars. The final victory of Sulla would witness the tomb of Marius being broken open and his corpse tossed into the Anio (Aniene), a tributary of the Tiber, by Sulla's soldiers (Cic. *Leg.* 2.56, Val. Max. 6.9.14, Plin. 7.54 §187). With its notorious excesses, Sulla's singular life story feels as though it could be the stuff of literature. (Bibi Saint-Pol/Wikimedia Commons/ Public domain)

Quintus Sertorius and the horse tail (Gorinchem, Stadhuis Gorinchem, RKDimages ID: 1267), oil on canvas (1638) by Gerard van Kuijl. The painting portrays Sertorius, who was famed for winning battles in Iberia against larger Sullan forces, illustrating to his Marian followers that a horse's tail could be picked out hair by hair but not pulled out all at once. Sertorius said to his men, 'By this illustration I have exhibited to you … the nature of the Roman cohorts. They are invincible to him who attacks them in a body; yet he who assails them by groups will tear and rend them apart' (Frontin. 1.10.1, cf. Plut. *Sert.* 16.3–4). Like Marius, whom he befriended and became an adherent of, Sertorius was a political outsider. His brilliant military exploits were later celebrated by Niccolò Machiavelli. (Alonso de Mendoza/Wikimedia Commons/Public domain)

precedent for this, it is extremely difficult to argue that Marius' appointment was unconstitutional. In 205 BC, having returned to Rome and the consulship (for which he was technically too young) after his splendid successes in Iberia, Publius Cornelius Scipio was setting up to invade Africa from Sicily when the Senate hesitated on giving him the green light. Livy (28.43) records that Scipio was quite prepared to go to the people if the Senate did not grant him Africa as his consular province.

Metellus, however, was no Scipio, and despite being bitter, he accepted the change in command – in 88 BC the ruthless adventurer Sulla would not – and on his return to Rome he acquired the well-deserved cognomen *Numidicus* for his endeavours against Iugurtha (Vell.2.11.2). In 102 BC, he received the honour of the censorship.

As a matter of fact, Marius did not bring with him any new ideas on how to conduct or even win the war, but he did, on the other hand, realize that to combat the rolling maul of Iugurtha he would need more boots on the ground. To this end, therefore, he took the decision to invite the *capite censi* to serve in the legions. Non-propertied volunteers now opted to join the army, and, interestingly, the Senate raised no protest. Yet the fundamental nature of the Roman army was changed, transforming it from the traditional citizen militia composed of a cross-section of the Servian propertied classes into a semi-professional force recruited from the poorest elements of society. From now on these particular men saw the army as a means of escaping poverty, rather than a duty that came as an interruption to normal life. Marius created, without realizing it, a client army, bound to its general as its *patronus*. We will return to this later in this work.

On assuming command in Africa, Marius soon found that it was not so easy to end the fluid warfare of the Numidian semi-desert as he had boldly boasted back in Rome. Events now took an ugly turn, with Marius adopting a deliberate policy of terrorism, torching fields, villages, and towns, and butchering their inhabitants (Sall. *B Iug.* 91.6–7, 92.3; cf. 54.6, 55.4–6). Marius then conceived and planned a daring venture, a long march so as to spread the terror of Roman arms deep in the heart of the hostile Numidian back of beyond. His first goal was Capsa (Gafsa, Tunisia). Achieving complete surprise, Marius captured the town, burnt it, massacred the adult males, sold the rest into slavery, and divided the booty among his soldiers. The destruction was complete. Sallust himself calls the treatment meted out to Capsa a 'violation of the usages of war [*ius belli*]', but feebly excuses it as a necessary evil since 'the place was important to Iugurtha and hard for the Romans to reach' (*B Iug.* 92.1). This act of calculated cruelty certainly cowed the Numidians into evacuating many of their settlements, and those few that foolishly resisted were captured by assault and razed to the ground. The momentum of the war was now with Marius.

Marius then came within an inch of losing the war in a pitched battle not far from the Muluccha (Moulouya) River, which was well within Mauretania; Sallust (*B Iug.* 95.1) broadly hints that it was Marius' *quaestor*, Sulla, who saved the day. We can be fairly certain that Sulla wrote his version of events in his *commentarii*. They are lost, but Sallust read them and made use of them in writing his account of the war.

In the end, Sulla befriended Bocchus, the vacillating king of the Mauri and father-in-law of Iugurtha, skilfully playing on the king's ambitions and fears. What followed was Sulla's spectacular desert crossing, which culminated in Iugurtha's betrayal and capture (Sall. *B Iug.* 113.4–7, Plut. *Sull.* 3.3, *Vir. ill.* 75.2). This spot of family treachery thus terminated a long-running war full of betrayals, skirmishes, and sieges. Sulla had a depiction of the episode engraved on a signet ring, provoking 'the hot and jealous temper of Marius' (Plut. *Mar.* 10.4, cf. Plin. 37.1.9).[1] Nevertheless, Marius was the hero of the hour. On 1 January 104 BC, he triumphed on the very day he entered his second consulship (Sall. *B Iug.* 114.3).

The war with Iugurtha had been a rather pointless, dirty affair, not so much in itself, but in the alleged corruption and incriminations of various kinds found and exchanged among the ruling classes of Rome (Sallust's monograph *Bellum Iugurthine*, for all its narrow major theme, provides an excellent 'portrait of an age'). The king was publicly humiliated and then thrown naked into the Mamertine Prison in Rome, where he starved to death six days later (Plut. *Mar.* 12.3–4, cf. Sall. *B Iug.* 113.6, Liv. *Per.* 67.4). The Senate, however, did not annexe Numidia, giving instead the western half of the kingdom to Bocchus as the price of his treachery, and the eastern half to Gauda, the weak-minded half-brother of Iugurtha. Yet it had made Marius' reputation and kick-started Sulla's career – as Sallust tells us (*B Iug.* 96.1), and Plutarch confirms (*Sull.* 2.2), Sulla did no military service in his youth. More than that, it saw Marius and Sulla fall out over who was responsible for the successful conclusion to this bitter conflict, a protracted quarrel that was to cast a long sanguinary shadow on Rome.

1 In 56 BC, Sulla's son Faustus minted a coin (*RRC* no. 426/1) depicting the scene of Iugurtha's capture.

OPPOSING FORCES

THE NORTHERN TRIBES

Once the Teutones who came from the remote shores of the Oceanus Germanicus overran all parts of Gaul

Saint Jerome, *Epistulae* 123.8

Most wars are the result of history distorted and harnessed to the cause of some individual or group goal, greed, or pride. Certainly, those for war shout loudest, eager for weapons to be whetted and men to be mustered. In this respect, nothing is more disastrous than giving history primacy over geography. History is subjective and selective: geography is truly the queen of sciences. The politically savvy – and glory-seeking – Caesar may have looked at the map but decided recent history was a better bet when it came to blatantly boost both his power and his profile.

Caesar's uncle had saved the Italian peninsula from the threatened invasion of the Cimbri and the Teutones, whose victories inflicted on earlier Roman commanders echo ominously in the background of the *commentarii*;

but the vivid memory of the near-disaster remained. Barbarian migrations were the stuff of Roman nightmares, and for nearly 14 years Rome lived under the mordant shadow of the wandering Germani. Caesar made good use of this deep-seated neurosis by playing up the 'Germanic menace' (*B Gall.* 1.33.3, 40.5, cf. 2.4.2–3; Plut. *Caes.* 26.1). But Caesar's propaganda also implied that he himself was the new Marius who could save Rome. With the Gallic War, Caesar put this view to the test. War is a good time to bury scruples, and he was no different.

Terror Cimbricus

Words have meaning, and Caesar was particularly adept in fighting information wars, turning half-truths into an art form. There was a calculating quality to Caesar's polemics. For instance, his assessment of the Gallic political scene – Gaul would have to become Roman or it would be overrun by the fierce, warlike Germanic race – was a gross hyperbole, but as a justification to spark his conquest of Gaul it would have convinced many who remembered the panic of five decades before. This was a transparent fig leaf for what was nothing more than a war of brute imperialism and personal aggrandizement. There may have been some clear signs of queasiness in the Senate, but the simplistic idea that Caesar was peddling to his audience there within was the hoary tale of 'us versus them'. It was (and still is) an easy one to sell and it gains traction. It did not matter that Caesar's replacement accusations lacked any empirical basis. Deep down, many people knew this, but people can grow accustomed to stories painting minorities and neighbouring nations as the perfect common enemy, glorifying past wars, and sowing fear. Caesar was a propagandist, albeit one with considerable talent and flair, and family history was the wellspring for his propaganda.

Much as I share the scepticism of (the famously anti-war) Leo Tolstoy about the individual's impact on history, to a significant extent this was going to be Caesar's war. When Caesar rolled the wild dice of war, he was perhaps thinking that his imperial enterprise was a dead cert. For Caesar, contradiction stimulated him, aggression galvanized him. After all, here was a man caught up in the 'logic of war', who acted accordingly. Be that as it may, he was to learn the high cost of conquering unwilling peoples. In launching his war on the Gauls, Caesar overlooked the utility of violence in remarking identities. Human beings tend to draw more closely to whatever identity is currently under threat. But that is not our purpose here. Our current interest lies in the aforementioned Cimbrian War, which was to be his uncle Marius' war.

The ominous peril from the north

For reasons lost to time, the Cimbri and the Teutones decided to leave their home territory on the western flank of the Cimbricus Chersonesus (Jutland peninsula) and migrate en masse southwards, carrying with them their entire families and movable possessions. The vagaries of the weather, disease, crop failure, overpopulation – any number of catastrophes may have swept away their livelihoods, which were their homes and their heritage, too. Elbowing other tribes out of the way wherever they wandered, both tribes were seeking land and a chance to settle, but with little idea where their journey might eventually lead. Archaeologists, on the other hand, have not discovered any clear indications of a mass migration from the Jutland peninsula in the early Iron Age.

These coastal lands were within the Germanic tribal realm, leading some scholars to believe that the Cimbri and Teutones were Germanic tribes. However, the names of their chieftains were Celtic (e.g. Boïorix), leading others to believe they were Celtic tribes. One explanation is that the Graeco-Roman authors were not familiar with the Germanic tribes and transmitted their names in the more familiar Celtic form. These authors themselves were divided in opinion whether the two tribes were Germanic or Celtic in origin.

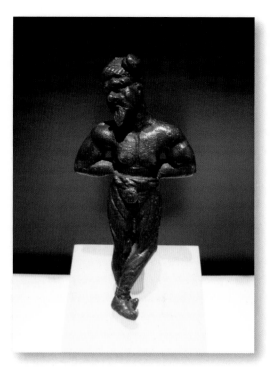

Bronze Roman ornament (Wien, RömerMuseum, inv. 21, 1991) depicting a shackled Germanic warrior. Found at the Roman military base of Vindobona, just north of what is now the centre of Vienna, and dated 2nd century AD, the figurine is shown wearing the tight woollen breeches – secured at waist and ankles by rawhide thronging – typical of Germanic warriors. Few warriors had armour or helmets: for defence, they depended on their shield and agility. His hair is combed and tied into a Suebian knot. Tacitus says the fashion spread to other Germanic tribes, though 'it is rare and confined to the period of youth' (*Germ.* 38.2). The Germani had no collective consciousness of themselves as a separate people, nation, or group of tribes. There is no evidence that they even called themselves 'Germani' or their land 'Germania'. (Gryffindor/ Wikimedia Commons/ CC-BY-SA-3.0)

Early Iron Age migrations of Northerners

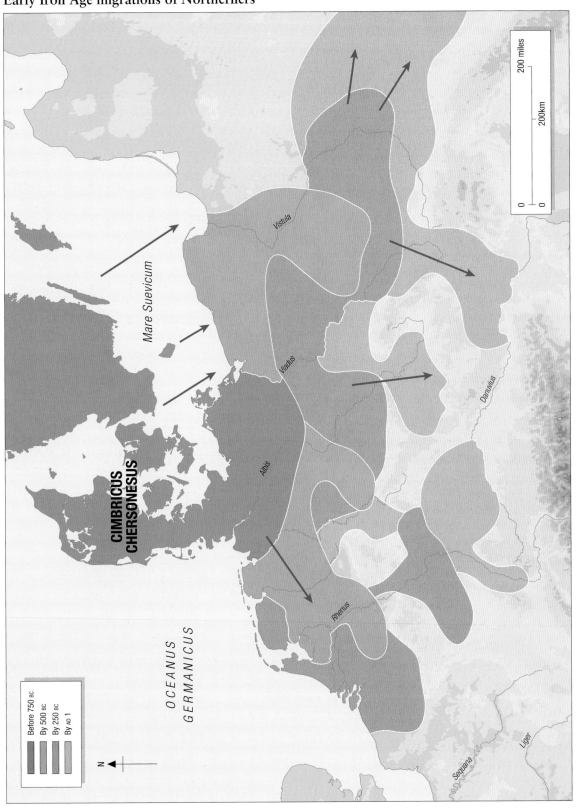

CIMBRICUS
CHERSONESUS

Mare Suevicum

Vistula

Viadus

Albis

Danubius

Rhenus

OCEANUS
GERMANICUS

Sequana

Liger

200 miles

200km

0

0

Before 750 BC
By 500 BC
By 250 BC
By AD 1

N

Photograph taken on 15 February 2017 from the International Space Station (NASA Photo ID ISS050-E-51156) as it passed over the Kingdom of Denmark. The west coast of the long Jutland peninsula (Cimbricus Chersonesus) is in plain view, the original homeland of the Cimbri and the Teutones. Tacitus describes Jutland as the 'sleeve or peninsula of Germania … the home of the Cimbri, who dwell nearest the Oceanus [Germanicus]' (*Germ.* 37.1). Florus relates that 'the Oceanus [Germanicus] had inundated their territories' (1.38.1) and the resulting deluge drove the two tribes to seek new lands elsewhere. Strabo, on the contrary, calls this reason for their wandering 'a fabrication' (7.2.1), and in the low-lying areas along the North Sea, as archaeology confirms, Iron Age villages were situated atop artificial mounds as a measure against flooding. On the map of the astronomer-geographer Ptolemaios (2.11.7), the *Kímbroi* are placed on the northernmost part of the peninsula. (Image courtesy of the Earth Science and Remote Scanning Unit, NASA Johnson Space Center)

So, who were these Northerners? The Teutones are first mentioned in the late 4th century BC by Pytheas, an intrepid navigator from the Greek colony of Massalia (Marseille). His work *Perì toū Okeanoū* has not survived, but according to Pliny (37.11 §35) Pytheas spoke of the Teutones (Gk. Τεύτονες) as inhabiting somewhere along the northern Oceanus coast of Europe. The Cimbri, on the other hand, do not enter the historical record until our period of study. Strabo (4.4.3, 7.1.3), Tacitus (*Germ.* 37.1, *Hist.* 4.73), and Pliny (4.28 §99) describe both peoples as Germanic, as do Caesar (*B Gall.* 1.33.3–4) and Augustus (*RG* 26.4). Appianus (*B civ.* 1.29, *Illyr.* 1.4), on the other hand, clearly distinguishes the Cimbri from the Germani, and along with Florus considers them to be a Celtic people, Florus explaining that the Cimbri, along with the Teutones and Tigurini, were 'fugitives from the extreme parts of Gaul' (1.38.1). Likewise, Sallust views them as 'Gauls' (*B Iug.* 114.3). On the other hand, the late-antique Christian writer Orosius hedges his bets by saying, 'the Cimbri, Teutones, Tigurini, and Ambrones, Gallic and Germanic tribes … formed a conspiracy to destroy the Roman empire' (5.16.1).

'As many men, so many opinions,' was the famous remark by the lawyer Hegio in Terence's *Phormio* (Act II, Scene 4), a comic play first staged at the *Ludi Romani* in 161 BC. Quite true, but Plutarch (*Mar.* 11.3) writes that the *communis opinio* was that the Cimbri and Teutones were Germanic tribes, and many authors like him frequently quoted them together (e.g. *Teutonos Cimbrosque*, Caes. *B Gall.* 2.4.1). Having said that, however, the matter of ethnicity is one still open to doubt, and remains a vexed question that divides scholars.

Celtic and Germanic are complicated terms. The idea of unified cultures is a convenient myth: instead, aspects of their respective art and technology were shared over wide areas among diverse cultures. Few, if any, of these peoples would even have identified themselves as Celtic or Germanic. Consequently, neither Celtica nor Germania resembled anything we might recognize today as a true country or even a tribal confederation. Rather, these were loose groupings of language and culture, within which individual tribes were often in rivalry or at war, frequently over land and resources.

Much of Germania, for instance, and many of its inhabitants were absolutely mysterious to the Romans. The sun of Mediterranean lands was bright, the air was clear, the silhouette of the hills was sharp, and the woods were open and thin. From the Roman perspective Tacitus best sums it up by asking his sophisticated audience the rhetorical question: 'Who would want to go to Germania, with its misshapen landscape and harsh climate?', and later throws in for good measure the indifferent verdict that Germania is little more than 'a land of bristling forests and unhealthy marshes' (*Germ.* 2.2, 5.1). For the most part, Tacitus' topographical appraisal of Germania consists of three recurring features: sinister forests, fetid swamps, and sacred groves. The Germani whom Tacitus describes have left us no literary record; but decades of archaeological investigations within modern Germany make it clear that Iron Age Germania was far from an impenetrable wilderness devoid of industry and agriculture, nor was it empty of settlements.

Graeco-Roman sources do portray the Celts as more advanced than the Germani, a belief confirmed by archaeology: the former were now raising stone ramparts, minting coins, manufacturing metalwork of finest artistry, and making appreciable advances in arms and armour. Additionally, the influence of the Celtic world on the material culture of Germania is evident in the material record at several levels, and the most spectacular contacts with the world of La Tène craftsmanship are evident in a number of prestigious items found in what was northern Germania. The best known of these is the gilded silver cauldron found in a peat bog near Gundestrup in north Jutland. With its symbols of fertility and war, life and death, and its beauty, this ritual object was the creation of an eastern Celtic master based in the Balkans sometime during the late 2nd century BC. The cauldron likely found its way to the Cimbricus Chersonesus via trade, taken there as war booty, or given as a gift. A cauldron, we are told by Strabo, was the most sacred vessel of the Cimbri, a fitting gift for Augustus himself, 'with a plea for his friendship and for an amnesty for their past offences' (7.2.1).

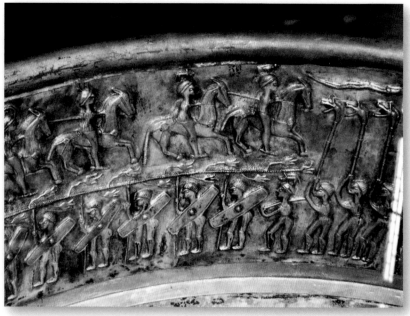

A word of caution is required with regards to our literary sources, however, particularly when on the subject of the Germani. It is wise to keep in mind the familiar prejudices and stereotyping of Graeco-Roman authors, where imagined belief in the moral inferiority of 'barbarians' (think Aristotle) is commonly contradicted by appreciation for the 'noble savage' (think Rousseau). True to form, Tacitus, who is rightly regarded as the greatest of Roman historians, praises the Germani for manliness, strength, stamina, chastity, fidelity, and other dignified traits. While probably true for the most part, this was a romanticizing device by which Tacitus could castigate his fellow Romans for addiction to soft living and loss of morality, as opposed to the strong, chaste, clean practices that were considered to have once belonged to a bygone age.

ROMAN: MARIUS' MULES

It is more a subject of joy that we have so few of the desperate characters which compose modern regular armies. But it proves more forcibly the necessity of obliging every citizen to be a soldier. This was the case with the Greeks and Romans, and must be that of every free state.

Thomas Jefferson to James Monroe, 19 June 1813

Marius' mules – (*muli Mariani*) as his soldiers were jokingly called (Plut. *Mar.* 13.1, Frontin. 4.1.7, Fest. 267 L) – did not constitute a proper professional army – that would come in 13 BC when Augustus made the army strictly professional (Dio 54.25.6) – but they did experience one military campaign after another, either in Africa, against the Numidians, or against invading northern tribes in the *provinciae* of Gallia Transalpina and Gallia Cisalpina. In reality, most of the rank and file served in only a limited number of campaigns, preferring a temporary time in the army and hoping for, as we shall discuss, some enhancement of their economic status after their return

ABOVE LEFT
Detail from a full-scale replica (Saint-Germain-en-Laye, Musée d'archéologie nationale) of the Gundestrup Cauldron (Copenhagen, Nationalmuseet), discovered by peat cutters in Rævemose near Gundestrop, north Jutland (1891). Seen here is one of the seven interior plates, showing (upper register) a procession of Celtic horsemen (chiefly nobles), and (lower register) a procession of armed warriors, the last of which wears a helmet with a crest in the form of a wild boar. (© Esther Carré)

ABOVE RIGHT
Terracotta statuette (Oxford, Ashmolean Museum), dated 2nd century BC, of a warrior sporting a distinctively Celtic hairstyle, drooping moustache, trousers, and tunic, along with a sheathed, long slashing sword, and a shield. Strabo says 'the equipment [of the Gauls] is in keeping with the size of their bodies, they have a long sword hanging at their right side, a long shield, and a spear in proportion' (4.4.3). (Carole Raddato/Wikimedia Commons/ CC-BY-SA-2.0)

to civilian life. As in the past, the officers considered time with the army as a necessary stage in their political careers (*cursus honorum*), not as an alternative to it.

The pre-Marian legion

At the beginning of our timespan, the legion was still organized, as it had been in Hannibal's day, into 30 tactical units. These were the maniples (*manipulus*, pl. *manipuli*), ten for each of the three distinct battle lines (*triplex acies*), which constituted the habitual battle formation. Polybios describes the manipular system of his day as follows: the first two lines, the *hastati* ('spearmen') and the *principes* ('chief men'), were composed of ten maniples, each maniple consisting of two centuries (*centuriae*). The third line, the *triarii* ('third-rank men'), was composed of ten maniples with only one century (*centuria*) each. A *centuria* was, at least on paper, 60-legionaries strong. The legion included 1,200 lightly armed legionaries (*velites*), who formed a screen in front of the formation, and to them was given the initiation of battle. The shower of javelins they let fly – each was armed with five (Lucilius

Satires 7.290) or seven (Liv. 26.4.4) – might open a breach in the opposing ranks; at least, it would expose weak points in the enemy formation that the heavier legionaries could exploit. It was the *pila* (much heavier missiles) and swords of these legionaries that determined the outcome of the battle. In all, on paper a manipular legion was 4,200-men strong (1,200 *hastati*, 1,200 *principes*, 600 *triarii*, 1,200 *velites*). The pre-Marian legion was supported by 300 citizen cavalry, too (Polyb. 6.19–26).

In the manipular legion, the distribution among the *triplex acies* was based on age, wealth, and experience. Each legionary being responsible for his own war gear, the *velites* were the poorest recruits, and, since their task was based entirely upon speed and mobility, they were also young and agile soldiers. The rest of the formation was distributed strictly according to age and experience. The legionaries of the first line, the *hastati*, were the youngest, while the third, the *triarii*, were the most-experienced soldiers. As Colonel Charles Ardent du Picq, who was mortally wounded by a stray Prussian shell on 15 August 1870, said in his analysis of the tactics employed by the army of Republican Rome:

> In the order by maniples in the Roman legion, the best soldiers, those whose courage had been proved by experience in battle, waited stoically, kept in the second and third lines. They were far enough away not to suffer wounds and not to be drawn in by the front line retiring into their intervals. Yet they were near enough to give support when necessary or to finish the job by advancing.
>
> Du Picq (2006: p. 65)

The manipular legion was suited to one style of fighting, at which it excelled. This was the straightforward, larger-scale actions where discipline, drill, and command and control became more important but involved little or no prior tactical manoeuvres. It was this sort of pitched battle that characterized most of what the Romans and their enemies, habitually denizens of the Mediterranean world, were used to in the 3rd and 2nd centuries BC. Although the decline of the manipular legion was part of a prolonged and not necessarily linear evolutionary process, it is possible to identify as a major catalyst the military humiliations of the last decade and a half of the 2nd century BC (at the hands of the Scordisci, Iugurtha of Numidia, and the antagonists of this monograph, the Cimbri and the Teutones, who, as we shall discover, had a nasty habit of devouring Roman manipular legions). Marius' reforms were to produce an army capable of effectively fighting a war of choice.

Sculptural relief (Selçuk, Efes Arkeoloji Müzesi) in marble showing a *lanista* armed with a stout baton – to encourage slackers. Crucial to the development of the spectacle of gladiatorial combat were the *lanistae*. They were indispensable operators who functioned as slave traders, managers, trainers, and impresarios all in one. Still, they were seen by their fellow citizens as utterly contemptible, somewhat like an unpleasant cross between a butcher and a pimp. It was such 'unsavoury' characters that Rutilius turned to so as to train his legionaries in swordplay. (© Nic Fields)

Proletarian army

Caius Marius has often been credited with taking the decisive steps that led the way to the professional standing army of the Principate – which, no matter the opposition standing opposite, (almost) won in the end. Rome, by the time Marius had come on the scene, was the dominant power in the Mediterranean basin, since such few states in the area that retained their autonomy did so by Rome's leave. Consequently, the annual levying of what was in effect a part-time citizen militia was incompatible with the running and maintenance of a carnivorous world empire. Moreover, wars had become drawn out, distant, and difficult, and these had turned out thousands of trained soldiers, many of whom would have found themselves strangers to civilian life after their long service overseas. The army had been their life and Marius called them back home. But besides these time-expired veterans, Marius also enrolled another more numerous kind of volunteer: the men with nothing, the *proletarii*.

Roman citizens not registered in one of the five Servian property classes – that is to say, those men who could not declare to the censors the minimum census qualification for enrolment in Class V – were excluded from military service. Lacking the means to provide themselves arms and armour, the *proletarii* were listed in the census simply as numbers, the *capite censi* or 'head count' (Val. Max. 3.3.1, Gell. 16.10.10). When levying his consular army for the ongoing struggle against Iugurtha, Marius drew upon 'the bravest soldiers from Latium – men who had either served under him or been recommended to him – and by personal appeals induced time-expired veterans to join his expeditionary force' (Sall. *B Iug.* 84.2). Yet, not content with just relying upon old-timers, he also employed another method of enlistment: Marius opened the ranks of his army to willing volunteers drawn from the *proletarii* of Rome:

Meanwhile [Marius] continued to sign soldiers, not, in accordance with traditional custom, from the propertied classes [viz. classes I–V], but accepting any man who volunteered – members of the *proletarii* for the most part. Some said he did this because he could not get enough of a better kind; others, that he wanted to curry favour with men of low condition, since he owed to them his fame and advancement. And indeed, if a man is ambitious for power, he can have no better supporters than the poor, for they are not concerned about their own

Funerary stele (Aquileia, Taberna Marciani) of the gladiator Quintus Sossius Albus, a *murmillo*. He is armed with *gladius* and *scutum*, the trademark weaponry of a legionary. (© Esther Carré)

possessions, for they have none, and whatever puts something into their pockets is right and proper in their eyes.

Sall. *B Iug.* 86.2–3

Sallust was not an uncritical admirer of Marius, and he sets out the two different explanations offered at the time for Marius' motives. Some argued that it was a response to the dearth of propertied citizens, while others saw Marius pandering to the poor for political reasons.

In addition, Sallust's comments on Marius' new recruits are illustrative. As Sallust makes clear, others than *capite censi* were also allowed to volunteer rather than wait for the incidence of a formal levy (*dilectus*). Still, of all the reforms attributed to Marius, the opening of the army ranks to the *capite censi* in 107 BC has obviously attracted the most attention, and the unanimous disapproval of ancient writers who accuse Marius of paving the way for the anarchic, avaricious soldiery whose activities were thought to have contributed largely to the fall of the Republic a few generations later.

Yet we should not accept as obviously true that Marius turned the army into an agent of revolution, for if we choose to do so, then we have to conveniently ignore the detail that he was not the first to enrol the *capite censi*. Earlier, in times of crisis to raise an army quickly, the Senate had impressed them, along with convicts, freedmen, and slaves, for service as legionaries (Rich 1983: pp. 329–30). In the aftermath of the devastating defeats at the Trebbia (218 BC), Lake Trasimene (217 BC), and Cannae (216 BC), the Senate made the first of a number of alterations to the Servian constitution. In the dark days following Cannae, for instance, two volunteer legions were raised using 8,000 able-bodied slaves purchased and armed by the state (Liv. 22.57.11, cf. 23.32.1). A fragment of speech apparently delivered in 171 BC by the elder Cato refers to the recruitment of 'the poor and *proletarii*'.[2] The 'proletarianization' of the army had been in process for some time. Marius was merely carrying one stage further a process visible during the 2nd century BC, by which the prescribed property qualification for service in the army was eroded and became less meaningful. By wiping away a *de jure* arrangement, the only real prerequisites were that of Roman citizenship and a readiness to soldier for the state.

Noticeably, the ancient sources, unlike modern commentators, do not say that Marius swept away the property qualification, or changed the law on eligibility. On the contrary, he merely appealed to the *capite censi* for volunteers, whom he could equip from state funds under the legislation drawn up by Caius Sempronius Gracchus, as tribune of the plebs in 123 BC, by which the state was responsible for equipping the soldier fighting in its defence. Even before Gracchus' *lex militaria*, there had been a progressive debasement of the property threshold for Class V from the earliest recorded qualification of 11,000 *asses* (Liv. 1.43.7) to 400 *drachmae* (equivalent to 4,000 *asses*) by the time of Polybios (6.19.2). At a later point, perhaps in 123 BC by Gracchus himself, the property qualification was reduced again, the minimum being set at 1,500 *asses* (Cic. *Rep.* 2.40). This last represents a very

Exercise sword made of hardwood (Haltern am See, Westfälisches Römermuseum) from the Roman fortress at Oberaden built by Nero Claudius Drusus in the autumn of 11 BC (Dio 54.33.4). It was once used for the training of legionaries. Trained to use the *gladius* to its best effect, recruits would practise against a 6-Roman-feet-high wooden post (1.78m), the *palus* common to gladiators (Juvenal 6.247), at which they would shuffle and lunge and cut and thrust. The use of an exercise sword greatly increased the range of practice, and even hardened veterans of countless battles were supposed to submit themselves to the punishing ordeal of bouts with dummy swords. (Marco Prins/ Livius.org/CC0 1.0)

---

2 E. Malcovati, *Oratorum Romanorum Fragmenta*[2] (Turin, 1955), p. 58, no. 152: '*expedito pauperem plebeium atque proletarium*'.

Roman re-enactors of *legio XV* training at the *palus* with dummy weapons at Hainburg-Carnuntum. According to Vegetius (1.11), the wickerwork shields and wooden swords given to recruits were double weight, a sure-fire method to increase their strength and stamina. The exercises with post and swords were based on the system in force at the training schools for gladiators. (MatthiasKabel/Wikimedia Commons/CC-BY-SA-3.0)

Based on a Celtic design, the Montefortino helmet was basically a hemispherical bowl beaten to shape, and mass-produced for the arming of soldiers by the state. It had a narrow peaked neck-guard and an integral crest knob, which was filled with lead to secure a crest pin. Such helmets frequently had large, scalloped cheek-pieces, as does this 3rd-century BC example (Bologna, Museo Civico Archeologico di Bologna, inv. 28233). It comes from the burial (Benacci tomba 953) of a Cisalpine Gaulish warrior. (© Esther Carré)

small amount of property indeed, almost certainly insufficient to maintain a family, but the effect was an ongoing attempt to increase the number of citizens that qualified for military service (Gabba 1976: pp. 7–10).

It is highly likely that those farming such diminutive plots, often merely 7 *iugera* (1.75ha) and often featuring in literary discussions about rural poverty (Val. Max. 4.4.6–7, 11; cf. Liv. 3.26.7, 42.34.2), would need additional paid work to supplement the household income. Still, this 7-*iugera* plot was very much the traditional figure for many of the *viritim* ('man-by-man') grants handed out by the state during the first half of the 2nd century BC: for context, that is nearly the size of two international rugby union fields. There was to be a slight increase in the following century. Caesar's *lex Iulio de agro Campano* of late April 59 BC is a good example. This bill stipulated that colonists drawn from families with at least three children would each receive a 10-*iugera* (2.5ha) plot in Campania (App. *B civ.* 2.10, Dio 38.7.3, Cic. *Att.* 2.16.1–2, 2.17.1, *Phil.* 2.39, Vell. 2.44.4, Suet. *Iul.* 20.3).

In short, Marius took a bold step and opened the ranks to *all* who wished to volunteer. It was the final step in a process initiated by Caius Gracchus, who allowed men of little property to be recruited. To include those with none was a logical conclusion of the process, something Rome's overseas ventures on increasingly far-flung fields had exacerbated. In reality, the result of Marius' reform was to legalize a process that had been present for about a century and that the Senate had failed to implement, that is, to open up the army to all citizens regardless of their property, arm them at state expense, and recruit them not through the *dilectus* but on a volunteer basis. Nonetheless, his rational reform would bode ill for the future of the Republic.

The penultimate step

Bred lean and resilient in the vicissitudes of daily survival at subsistence level, Marius would have much preferred volunteers who were members of the rural population. This was for the simple reason that such men were rightly considered to be better material for soldiering than their urban counterparts, at best a rough and undernourished lot. Yet these urbanites, the men with nothing, were willing to join for any number of reasons. While it was not high, there was regular pay, and there was an ordered life, decent food and clothing, and, perhaps, the chance of improving one's lot. So, only too grateful to escape the filth and fickleness of urban life and the desire for a life free of routine drudgery all played their part in attracting the *proletarii*; poverty was the prime cause for their abandonment of civilian life. These men were enrolled in the army by Marius on his own initiative to make up the numbers in his army destined for bitter war in Africa. With Marius the pattern was set whereby the volunteer followed his general, often identifying his fortunes with him. But this would be a race that was a marathon, not a sprint.

What was new about Marius dropping the property qualification for army enlistment was that it was never reimposed thereafter. This would later open the way for ambitious and unscrupulous politicians to turn the poorest of Rome's citizens into their own clients by the promise of obtaining land distributions for them on discharge. That is why the aforementioned agrarian law of Caesar would cater not only for urban poor, but Pompeian veterans too, who just happened to be in Rome and helped to assure the passage of the bill. But this promise of land came to constitute a precedent for the future whereby soldiers looked to their general rather than the state for the rewards of service, above all a grant of land on their demobilization. Simultaneously, a general looked to his discharged veterans to support him in the cutthroat arena of Roman politics. The mutual interdependence between general and soldiers at the conclusion of a war meant that, in any case, the general would be anxious to attach to himself so many clients, while they were clearly concerned to secure for themselves as much as possible.

And so it was that volunteers from the *proletarii* of Rome chose to join the legions, 'imagining that they would make a fortune out of the spoils' (Sall. *B Iug.* 84.4) – and certainly, serving under Marius in Numidia with regard to material rewards, their hopes were to be fulfilled (Sall. *B Iug.* 87.1, 91.6, 92.2). Meanwhile, the Senate, despite assuming that Marius as consul would levy the soldiers by the normal and constitutional channel of raising an army by means of the *dilectus* based on the census, raised no protest. It was a simple step, revolutionary only in that Marius created, without realizing it,

Montefortino helmet discovered in the Rhône in 1969, dated to around 100 BC, and an Augustan-period 'Mainz'-type *gladius* excavated at Saintes-Maries-de-la-Mer in 1998 (Arles, Musée de l'Arles et de la Provence antiques, inv. X-16069, inv. X-15990). The 'Mainz' pattern of *gladius Hispaniensis*, with its exceptionally long stabbing point, was little changed since its adoption from the Iberians at the time of the First Punic War. (Ad Meskens/Wikimedia Common/CC-BY-SA-3.0)

29

Full-scale reconstruction of late Republican Roman Montefortino helmet (Alise-Sainte-Reine, MuséoParc Alésia). One of the commonest designs throughout the Italian peninsula, the Montefortino helmet offered good protection against downward blows. Large cheek-pieces protected the face without obscuring the wearer's vision or hearing. The type is named after the necropolis at Montefortino, Fermo Province, in central Italy. (© Esther Carré)

a type of client army, bound to its commander as its *patronus* because, as Plutarch lets on, 'contrary to law and custom he enrolled in his army poor men with no property qualifications' (Plut. *Mar.* 9.1), even though he was merely formalizing an existing unofficial practice (Sall. *B Iug.* 86.4). Marius was a pragmatist and was merely recognizing the status quo. For this reason we need not believe that the state was scrambling for manpower anywhere it could grab it, so opening the floodgates to the landless poor, or that the *dilectus* suddenly became obsolete overnight (Brunt 1971: pp. 403–10, 635–68; cf. Rich 1983). The final step would have to wait until Augustus.

Mutual interests

Still, volunteers from the *proletarii* from this time forward continued to be eligible for service, and probably comprised a considerable proportion of the army's annual requirements. These men, who had much more to fight for and much less to return to, understandably enlisted to better their economic circumstances. In particular, as previously alluded to, these men had a yen for land: on demobilization their hope was to metamorphose from serving soldiers into self-sufficient smallholders. And they were not to be disappointed: Marius' returning veterans, not only those who had served during his two Numidian campaigns, but those who would fight against the northern tribes, too, received land, mainly in Africa and Gallia Cisalpina (*Vir. ill.* 73, App. *B civ.* 1.29).

From 107 BC onwards, proletarian recruits signed up for the army with the hope that their generals would grant them pecuniary rewards at the termination of a campaign. In addition to the booty soldiers could gain from a war, the anticipation of tangible benefits in the form of land at the time of discharge became the motivation to serve, and this would gradually transform soldiering from a civic duty into a paying profession. Before long, another logical consequence was to follow: serving soldiers understood that a secure future post-service depended upon their general, the only one in a

THE ALTAR OF DOMITIUS AHENOBARBUS

The Altar of Domitius Ahenobarbus (the Paris–Munich Reliefs is the more accepted title) is a large rectangular plinth believed to have once stood outside a temple to Neptune in the Circus Flaminius at Rome. One side (Paris, musée du Louvre, inv. Ma 975), seen here, shows a scene dominated by a sacrifice, the *suovetaurilia*, in which a sheep, pig, and bull are killed in honour of Mars to ensure purification. Just to the left of this scene is a tall, dashing figure in military garb, Mars himself. To his left two legionaries seem to stand guard while citizens are being registered, while to the right of the *suovetaurilia* two other legionaries stand idly chatting along with a cavalry trooper, who is calming his horse. (© Esther Carré)

The Altar of Domitius Ahenobarbus, as it is traditionally known, is a large rectangular base that acted as a plinth for a sculptural group. It is believed to have once stood outside a temple dedicated to Neptune in the Circus Flaminius at Rome (Stilp 2001). The temple itself was built or repaired at the expense of Cnaeus Domitius Ahenobarbus (*cos.* 32 BC), a senator-cum-*condottieri* who commanded a fleet of 50 ships in the Mare Ionium (Ionian Sea) for Marcus Brutus against the triumvirs and, having struck his flag, subsequently for Marcus Antonius, which greatly offended Octavianus. He was to switch sides once more, slipping stealthily in a small boat over to Octavianus on the very eve of Actium. The twofold turncoat died a few days afterwards (Vell. 2.76.2, 84.2, Dio 50.13.6, Suet. *Nero* 3.2, Plut. *Ant.* 63.6).

There is an *aureus* issued by Ahenobarbus, possibly dated to 41 BC, which depicts a tetra-style temple and carries the inscription NEPT(*unus*) CN(*aeus*) DOMITIVS L(*ucius*) F(*ilius*) IMP(*erator*). The temple is shown raised on a typical podium but without stair of approach, and on the obverse is the head of a heavyset, clean-shaven man inscribed AHENOBARB(*us*). The suggestion is that Ahenobarbus vowed to erect or restore the temple on the eve of his naval engagement with Cnaeus Domitius Calvinus (*cos.* 53 BC, *cos.* II 40 BC), for he was to be saluted as *imperator* by his marines and sailors after intercepting and destroying the Caesarian fleet. According to Appianus (*B civ.* 4.15), this rather sanguinary maritime affair, which saw the complete loss of *legio Martia*, took place on the very day the first battle of Philippi was fought (3 October 42 BC).

Three sides of the plinth, housed in the Glyptotek Munich (inv. 239), depict a marine cortège of sea nymphs and Tritons celebrating the nuptials of the god Neptune and the nymph Amphitrite. The fourth side (5.65m x 1.75m x 0.80m), made up of two pieces of marble and currently housed in the Louvre (inv. Ma 975), shows a scene of purification. The centre of this narrative scene is dominated by a sacrifice, the *suovetaurilia*. To the left is a figure in military garb; he wears a short muscled cuirass with two rows of fringed *pteruges*, a crested helmet, and greaves. He also has a circular shield, a spear, and a sword, which he wears on the left side. Around his waist is a sash knotted at the front with the loose ends tucked up at either side. Most probably he is Mars dressed as a military tribune.

To his left, two legionaries, in open-faced helmets and mail shirts, seem to stand guard while citizens are registered at a *dilectus*. One is shown carrying a *gladius Hispaniensis* suspended from his right hip. To the right of the central scene, two other legionaries, similarly equipped, stand at ease, along with a cavalry trooper, also in a *lorica hamata* but wearing a plumed Boiotian helmet, who prepares to mount his horse. The mail shirts of all four legionaries have clearly depicted, leather-backed doubling on their shoulders, and are belted at the waist to distribute part of the load onto the hips. All four also carry the dished oval *scutum* with barleycorn-shaped *umbones*. One of their helmets is a Montefortino type and the other three are of Etrusco-Corinthian pattern, an Italic derivative of the Corinthian helmet. They all have long horsehair crests hanging from the crown of their helmets. None of them are wearing greaves.

Naturally, there has been much discussion among scholars on the significance of the Altar, its original location, and most importantly, the date. For the present purpose, the arms and equipment of the soldiers on the fourth side attract special notice. Recent examination has suggested that this side is in a different marble from the rest. It is thus believed that the mythical seascape relief was imported, possibly reused, from a Hellenistic source, while the *dilectus* relief, decidedly low-key and much more down-to-earth, was specially commissioned. One convincing view places the Altar in the first decade of the 1st century BC, not long after Marius' army reforms, when Cnaeus Domitius Ahenobarbus' granduncle of the same name was consul in 96 BC and censor in 92 BC (Plin. 17.1.3). A man of violent temper, apparently his fellow censor the orator Lucius Licinius Crassus said of him, 'Should his bronze beard really surprise us? After all, he has an iron face and a heart of lead' (Suet. *Nero* 3.1).

Roman annalistic tradition has the penultimate king of Rome, Servilius Tullius (r. *c.* 579–*c.* 534 BC) introduce a major reform of its socio-political and military organization. His first consideration was the creation of a citizen army, and the most important point was to induce the citizens to adequately arm themselves for the defence of the state. So a census of all adult male citizens recorded the value of their property and divided them accordingly into five classes. The *iurator*, oath taker, on the Altar of Domitius Ahenobarbus (Paris, musée du Louvre, inv. Ma 975) records names and property holdings, either as a census or as part of the levying, *legio*, of citizen soldiers. This he does in a *codex*, made of two wooden *tabulae*, wax tablets. Six more of these *codices* can be seen at his feet. The figure sitting before the *iurator* is the censor. (© Esther Carré)

Fused remains of an iron mail-shirt (Saint-Germain-en-Laye, Musée d'archéologie nationale, inv. 71442) unearthed at Chalon-sur-Saône (*département* of Saône-et-Loire). Several Roman mail-shirts, usually rolled up as here, have been recovered from rivers such as the Saône. Roman mail-shirts came in two styles according to the place of origin, Gaul or the Hellenistic East. During the last century of the Republic, the first style was very popular with horsemen and the second had shoulder reinforcements modelled after those of the Greek *linothōrax*, which provided extra protection against downward sword strokes (a boon to those fighting on foot). Such shirts weighed around 9–15kg, depending on the body length and the number of rings – 30,000 minimum. (Esther Carré)

position to provide for them. This was at the root of the client and private armies that dogged the final decades of the dying Republic.

The political aspect of this move by Marius of enlisting soldiers on his own initiative is hardly less important. Though a piece of land appears to have been a more popular reward, a successful general did have the option of offering his demobilized veterans money for continued political support in Rome. Most of the men recruited by Marius undoubtedly were, or had been, members of the rural population (Sall. *B Iug.* 73.6, cf. Plut. *Mar.* 41.2, App. *B civ.* 1.67), and their idea of attainable riches was ownership of a smallholding. And there is little reason to doubt that those urban citizens aspired to landed property, too, especially individuals whose roots were rural and whose migration to the metropolis had been forced by economic hardship. At the conclusion of the Numidian campaign, they looked to their popular general for rewards other than the booty they had already acquired, that is to say, workable plots of land. There is no evidence that Marius actually promised his proletarian recruits land when he enlisted them, but as consul in 103 BC he set about providing it. So, while he was training his new army for the approaching showdown with the Cimbri and Teutones, he proposed an agrarian bill seeking land in Africa for the surviving veterans of the war with Iugurtha.

Marius' legislation would be pushed through by the brilliant but unscrupulous tribune of the plebs, Lucius Appuleius Saturninus, a demagogue with an agenda of his own who frequently resorted to mob violence, and even – it was rumoured – assassination to support his sinister strategy. We can, of course, argue that from now on soldiers turned to their generals and not the Senate for recompense, the case in point being when Sulla got his soldiers to march on Rome in 88 BC (App. *B civ.* 1.57, Plut. *Sull.* 9, *Mar.* 35.4). However, such a view is far too pessimistic, as not all soldiers would follow their general come what may. They would fight loyally in the defence of Rome, when it was under threat, and were bound by oath to follow their appointed commanders, but they had no commitment to a political system that did little for them.

While helping his veterans was Marius' goal, it ought to have been a goal of the Senate, too. Traditionally, the Senate had made no provisions for discharged soldiers, letting them drift back home after their service, often to sink into poverty. But periods of service had lengthened, and it could not be ruled out that soldiers might be mobilized for years on end. Moreover, wars of conquest took armies far afield, and being uprooted in this way certainly hampered their chances of being reabsorbed into civilian society. Marius fought to see that this would not happen to the veterans of his campaigns. But ultimately, it was the Senate that shirked this duty. It failed to recognize the new proletarian army for what it was: an organization with material interests and individual concerns.

It is probably true that throughout Rome's history, soldiers exhibited more loyalty towards a charismatic and competent commander such as Marius. Therefore, what we actually witness with him is not actually a change in the attitude of the soldiers, but a change in the attitude of the generals themselves. Judge this for yourself. In 202 BC, after the serious struggle at Zama, if he had harboured any revolutionary ideas, Scipio could have chosen to march on Rome at the head of his victorious, battle-tried veterans. If we return to Sulla and his first march on Rome, his officers were so appalled at his plan to steal power that all except one *quaestor* (most likely Lucius Licinius Lucullus) resigned on the spot. At the same time, his soldiers, though eagerly anticipating a lucrative campaign in the Hellenistic East, followed him only after he had convinced them that he had right on his side (likewise Caesar's soldiers crossed the Rubicon only after appeals on constitutional grounds). When envoys met Sulla on the road to Rome and asked him why he was marching on his native country, as Appianus points out, he replied: 'To deliver her from her tyrants' (*B civ*. 1.57). In other words, Sulla produced an unequivocal answer that ended with the all-purifying invocation of tyrannicide. As for Marius, it probably never even crossed his

Modern mail made of alternating rows of riveted and solid rings. Several patterns of linking the rings together have been attested, but the most common (and the dominant type in Europe) was the four-to-one pattern, where each ring was linked to four others, two in the row above and two in that below. With this complicated construction, the force of a sword blow was spread over a wide enough area for the wearer to be no more than bruised. The rings were made using wrought iron. The use of linked iron rings to forge a flexible form of body armour by the Romans stems from their having borrowed the idea from the Gauls, among whom it had been in use since the 3rd century BC, albeit reserved for the aristocratic warrior elites such as the Vachères warrior. Varro calls *lorica hamata* 'Gallic' (*de Lingua Latina* 5.116), acknowledging that the Romans acquired their knowledge of mail making from the Gauls, who, it seems, were also its original fabricators. (Roland zh/Wikimedia Commons/ CC-BY-SA-3.0)

mind at the time that the unscrupulous Sulla would do the unthinkable by mounting a military *coup d'état* and (if Sallust is to be credited) to corrupt military discipline (Sall. *Hist.* 1 fr. 79 Ramsey). After all, a proletarian army was not meant to be the private militia of the general who commanded it, but the embodiment of the oligarchic Republic at war.

Maximalist ends, minimalist means

Clausewitz – or at least the version of Clausewitz that is taught in many war academies – discussed the need to understand that the art of war was the use of the available means for the predetermined end. Equally, this connoisseur of causal explanations of events that facilitate evaluating means and ends, cautioned there must be a workable balance between these two paradigms in the war upon which one is embarking. The Achilles' heel, of course, is that militaries have an inherent habit of preparing to fight the war they want, not the one that the enemy visits upon them.

With regard to the Roman military effort in Numidia, there was, in short, a chronic lack of balance between ends and means. One problem was the fact that the Roman high command had initially treated the Numidian war merely as the same war in a different place. This was a toxic mix of *hubris* and denial. As they would discover to their cost, in the callous crucible of conflict, it was very much a different war in a different place. Since the need for change is rarely self-evident, militaries usually resist learning so long as

Full-scale reconstruction of Roman legionary *lorica hamata* (Alise-Sainte-Reine, MuséoParc Alésia). Although the mail was very laborious to make, the problem was partly overcome by the introduction of alternate rows of solid rings, which did not require being riveted. The 'rivet' to secure the flattened ends of riveted rings was a small triangular chip of metal, closed with a pair of tongs with recessed jaws. (© Esther Carré)

A *caliga* (Saint-Germain-en-Laye, Musée d'archéologie nationale, inv. 2257) from the site of the legionary fortress at Mainz-Mogontiacum. The standard form of military footwear for legionaries, *caligae* were heavy soled hobnailed footgear worn by all ranks up to and including centurions. Though they look to us like stout sandals, they were in fact marching boots. The open design allowed for the free passage of air (and water) and, unlike modern military boots, was specifically designed so as to reduce the likelihood of blisters during 'yomping' (the bane of all fighting soldiers), as well as other incapacitating foot conditions such as trench foot – a severe fungal infection caused by wearing wet boots over a long period.
(© Esther Carré)

they believe the existing way of doing business still works. Still, wars have a habit of educating and shaking militaries, especially if the existing way of doing business is shown to be obsolete. This was where Marius came in.

While Marius girded up for a trial of strength with the northern tribes, he made changes in the tactical organization of the legion: he abolished the maniple and substituted the cohort (*cohors*, pl. *cohortes*) as the standard tactical unit of the legion – or so he is credited with. On two occasions during Metellus' first Numidian campaign, Sallust (*B Iug.* 50.2, 51.3) uses the term *cohortes* and not *manipuli*. It is unclear whether or not this is an inconsistency on Sallust's part, for Marius is supposed to have introduced this change *after* the Iugurthine War, not during it. Likewise, *cohortes* of legionaries are referred to once more by Sallust (ibid. 100.4), this time during Marius' second Numidian campaign in 106 BC.

To be sure, no ancient text specifically attributes this major tactical reform to Marius. On the one hand, Sallust (*B Iug.* 100.2, 103.1) describes legionaries still deployed in the manipular fashion during Marius' second Numidian campaign. On the other hand, some scholars have detected in Sallust's account (*B Iug.* 49.6) of the earlier operations against Iugurtha, namely those conducted by Metellus, the last reference to maniples manoeuvring as the sole tactical unit of the battle line. All in all, and despite the obvious doubt, the most credible occasion for this reorganization would be during Marius' reforms of 104 BC, that is to say, in the course of his extensive preparations for the war against the northern tribes.

The principle of a part-time citizen militia was retained at Rome, long after states in the Mediterranean world had come to rely on soldiers who were primarily tough, disciplined professionals. As the Roman army became the architect of empire, on the other hand, the Romans modified the system to cope with the demands of wars that were being fought further and further from home, and so the intimate link between warfare and the agricultural year was eventually broken. Take, for instance, the matter of pay. From the beginning of the 4th century BC, Rome paid its citizen soldiers for the duration of a campaign (Liv. 5.7.12–13, Diod. 14.16.5). The wage was not high and certainly did not turn soldiering into a profession, but it just about supported the citizen during his military service by covering his basic living expenses. The Marian reforms in fact did not change the rate of pay, for a soldier still received five *asses* per day (cf. Polyb. 6.39.12), bare subsistence with deductions for rations and equipment.

Fighting the Northerners

Roman real strength lay in the set-piece battle, the decisive clash of opposing armies that settled the issue one way or another. Polybios saw the Romans as rather old-fashioned in their straightforward and open approach to warfare, commenting that as a race they tended to rely instinctively on 'brute force' (βίᾳ/*bía*, 1.37.7) when it came to making war. The former Achaean League *hipparchos* may have a point, but the Roman military was well suited to the short, high-intensity encounter. This was because of the deep cultural belief in Rome that only the destruction of the enemy's army by battle wins a war. In this regard, it has long been recognized that the battle of Pydna (168 BC), Aemilius Paulus against Perseus, was the triumph of the Roman maniple over the Macedonian phalanx, a thing of brutal terror, but not without vulnerability – more than 20,000 phalangites were cut to shreds that day (Liv. 44.42.7). Indeed, this tactical disposition was adequate until Rome came to meet an opponent whose war-fighting concepts and capabilities were radically different from the slow methodical advance of the phalanx with its 'bristling rampart of outstretched *sarissae*' (Plut. *Aem.* 19.1). The crucial difference, of course, was the fact that the northern barbarians were not like the royal armies of the Hellenistic world.

Le guerrier de Vachères (Avignon, musée lapidaire, inv. G 136c), a limestone statue dated to 1st century BC. It shows the characteristic mail-shirt of interlocking rings, heavy woollen cloak, tubular torc, and sword belt of the aristocratic Celtic warrior. A long slashing sword hangs at his right hip and he leans on his shield in characteristic Gaulish fashion. The sword was habitually suspended from a bronze or iron chain worn around the waist, which passed through a loop at the back of the scabbard. (Rvalette/Wikimedia Commons/Public domain)

A military nation and warlike peoples are not the same. The Germanic and Celtic peoples were warlike from audacity and instinct. Their principal tactic was to stake everything upon a vigorous onslaught at the start of the battle, beating down the shields of the opposition, breaking into their formation, and each warrior going after a single man. This was a terrifying thing, and at times could swiftly sweep away an adversary or annihilate him in the blink of an eye – especially a nervous one – but if it was halted, the warriors would tend to lose their enthusiasm and make a hasty retreat. To meet this brutal method of attack, where the perpetrators believed that fighting power increased in proportion to the size of the mass, the formation in three fixed battle lines of maniples was unsuited. The units themselves were small and shallow, and an attack strongly pressed home might easily overcome their resistance and induce a nerve-shredding collapse. In an engagement against the Celtic Insubres (225 BC), who were armed with long, blunt-ended, two-edged swords designed for downward slashing strikes, the *hastati* had attempted to circumvent this difficulty by substituting

Gaulish waist-belt of iron chain (Niort, Musée ethnographique et archéologique du Donjon) found at Faye-l'Abbesse (*département* of Deux-Sèvres), and dated to the beginning of La Tène period (La Tène A, 460–400 BC). Belts were often worn, particularly the waist-belt of the warrior, which was generally a chain of bronze or iron. As seen here, the belt was closed by engaging the hook in the ring. (© Esther Carré)

their *pila* for the thrusting spears (*hastae*) of the *triarii* stationed to their rear (Polyb. 2.33.4).[3]

It is in battle that a military organization justifies its existence. With its limited size of only two centuries, the maniple was at a distinct disadvantage when pitted against such a robust style of fighting as practised by the northern tribes. Marius, fully aware what the Romans were up against, probably asked himself the key question: 'How do we fight tomorrow?' His answer was to strengthen his front line of defence by increasing the size of the individual units. With the cohort taking the place of the maniple as the basic tactical unit, the cohortal legion was organized into ten cohorts of equal size, strength and purpose. Naturally, with the lowering of the property qualification and its eventual abolition, legionaries were now uniformly equipped by the state at public expense. Consequently, variations in war gear originally linked to differing property classes now ceased to have any *raison d'être*.

In effect, the cohort was essentially a triple grouping of a maniple of *hastati*, a maniple of *principes,* and a maniple of *triarii* (*velites* were abolished), one behind the other as before but no longer separated into three thin lines. With ten cohorts – each of which was subdivided into six centuries – forming a cohortal legion, Marius had essentially cut the battle array of the manipular legion into ten slices from front to back. Being a large but manageable unit, the uniformly armed and sized *cohortes* could be deployed anywhere, unlike the *manipuli* they had replaced, which had been restricted to fixed positions. In its day, the manipular legion had been a formidable battlefield opponent, yet the cohortal legion, with its internal structure of *cohortes* and *centuriae*, had far greater tactical flexibility and staying power.

With the increase in size of the basic tactical unit from 120 to 480 men (thereby implying a legion of 4,800), the maniple had had its day. Confusingly, it may seem, Festus, a Latin grammarian writing in the late 2nd century AD, notes that 'after Marius' (453 L) the legion was 6,200-men

---

3   It is worth noting that the term *hastati* (spearmen) should be taken to mean armed with throwing spears (*pila*) instead of thrusting ones (*hastae*). This is after all the sense it bears out in our earliest surviving example of it, in Ennius' line *hastati spargunt hasti*, 'hastati who hurl hasti' (*Annales* fr. 284 Vahlen), and their name probably reflects a time when they alone used *pila*.

strong, instead of the 4,000-man total (raised to 5,000 in emergencies) which had previously been the norm (Polyb. 1.16.2, 2.24.13, 3.107.11, 6.20.9, 6.21.9–10; Liv.22.36.2, cf. 29.24.13). As Sallust makes plain, in 107 BC 'Marius set sail [for Africa] with a force considerably larger than that authorized by the [senatorial] decree' (*B Iug.* 86.4), which may be connected with Festus' statement if we are looking at the two legions a consul routinely levies. That all said, military historians often talk about the Roman legion as if it were one numerically homogenous unit. Conversely, in practice, legions were undoubtedly seldom up to their nominal strength, death, disease, and desertion all taking their grim toll. Even if we have assumed that the nominal strength of the Marian cohort was 480 men, the actual size of the Marian legion is a matter of controversy. On paper, it is likely that it averaged some 5,000 men all ranks, but the total complement could be higher (6,000) or, more likely, much lower (3,000). The literary sources confound the problem because, as Brunt (1971: pp. 687–93) elucidates, they normally multiply by 5,000 or so whenever they use the term *legio*. In other words, *legio* is equal to 5,000 regardless of actual size.

The cohort as a configuration of three maniples was not an entirely novel innovation, as the unit appears to have been in use as a tactical, as opposed to an administrative, expedient from the time of the Second Punic War. Polybios (11.23.1), in his account of the battle of Ilipa (206 BC), pauses at one point to explain the meaning of the term *cohors* (κοόρτις/*koórtis*) to his Greek readership. Again, in the fight against Indibilis, Polybios says Scipio 'led his main force from the camp in four *cohortes*' (11.33.1). Surprisingly, this three-maniple formation receives no mention in his mechanical discussion of army organization neither in the sixth book nor in his comparison of legion and phalanx in the 18th book, although, it should be stated, there is little on tactics in both these narratives. Perhaps, then, Scipio's formation was little more than a temporary expedient. He certainly did not retain this tactical disposition in the later battle against Hannibal at Zama (202 BC).

Electrum stater, Pictones 2nd/1st century BC (Paris, BNP Cabinet des Médailles) depicting a Gaulish warrior. He wears what looks like a mail-shirt with shoulder cape, belted at the waist. It is believed that the Romans first met mail-clad Gauls in Gallia Cisalpina. The Romans soon adopted this La Tène technology, and those citizens who had the means would naturally choose a mail-shirt (lorica hamata) over a bronze pectoral. With Marius' reforms, state-provided mail body armour became standard issue. (World Imaging/Wikimedia Commons/ CC-BY-SA-3.0)

Impedimenta

If Marius could not be credited with the original creation of the cohort, his reorganization of the army in the period 104–103 BC, while waiting for the northern tribes in Gallia Transalpina, perfected the system. What Marius certainly did was to improve the legion's mobility and independence of movement by getting rid of the mass of non-combatants who had traditionally followed the Roman armies: slaves who carried the equipment of soldiers, slave traders and other merchants looking for opportunities to enrich themselves, even prostitutes. Marius, who was disdainful of this mass of civilian parasites, although he may not have gotten rid of all of them, threw out of the army those who carried military equipment, transferred to the soldiers the care of their weapons and what was needed for campaigning, and reorganized the baggage train – pack animals or wagons if the terrain allowed them – as part of the legion and under supervision of slaves (*calones*).

From now on, as well as his arms and armour, each soldier was to carry his personal belongings, rations, cooking utensils, and the various tools necessary to build the marching camps which they habitually constructed each day with speed and completeness. All these ancillary items (*impedimenta*) were fastened to a T-shaped carrying pole (*furca*) which rested on their shoulders (Frontin. 4.1.7). The legionary, like all foot soldiers before his day and after, was grossly overloaded – alarmingly so, according to some accounts. Cicero, no lowly soldier he, writes the following on military service:

> [How] great the labour is of an army on its march; then consider that they carry more than half a month's provisions, and whatever else they may want: that they carry the burden of the stakes [for entrenchment], for as to shield, sword, or helmet, they look on them as no more encumbrance than their own limbs, for they say that arms are the limbs of a soldier, and those indeed they carry so commodiously, that when there is occasion they throw down their burdens, and use their arms as readily as limbs.

Cic. Tusc. 2.16.37

A *carnyx* (Chateau de Montbéliard, Musée archéologique) wrought in sheet bronze with a stylized boar's head, dated 2nd century BC, discovered at the *oppidum* of Epomanduodurum (*département* of Doubs). The hollow boar's head has an erect mane and ears rather like those depicted on the Gundestrup Cauldron or on the Arc de Triomphe, Orange. (Arnaud 25/Wikimedia Commons/CC-BY-SA-3.0)

Normally, perhaps, a legionary carried rations for three days, not the two weeks to which Cicero exaggeratingly refers to. Still, it has been estimated that the legionary was burdened with equipment weighing as much as 35kg, if not more. As Edward Gibbon justly said, this weight 'would oppress the delicacy of a modern soldier' (*Decline and Fall* I.1.28), that is, a soldier of his day.

Thus encumbered, legionaries now looked like beasts of burden and without doubt warranted their mocking moniker *muli Mariani*. This brings to mind one of the myriad military maxims attributed to Napoleon Bonaparte:

> There are five things which a soldier should never be without: his firelock, his ammunition, his knapsack, his provisions (for at least four days), and his entrenching tool. The knapsack may be reduced to the smallest size possible, if it be thought proper, but the soldier should always have it with him.

Military Maxims 59

It is interesting to note that Napoleon has recognized the requirement of every soldier to carry an entrenching tool. Our Roman legionary was now expected to carry a sickle (*falx*) for cutting grain and forage, a wicker basket

The bell of the *carnyx* (Edinburgh, National Museum of Scotland, inv. IL.2011.1.1), found (1816) in a peat bog near Deskford, Banffshire, dated AD 80/200. When found, it still retained a wooden tongue mounted on springs, which no doubt added to the cacophony when the instrument was blown. Originally, its eyes would have been of brightly coloured enamel. The Deskford *carnyx* ended its life as a sacrifice, a ritual offering to some unknown god. (© Esther Carré)

(*sporta*) for earth moving, along with either a pickaxe (*dolabra*) or an iron-shod wooden spade (*pala*) for breaking up earth, and a sharpened stake (*pilum muralis*) for fortifying the overnight marching camp.

The Roman army was a different military organization from that of 105 BC, when the Romans entered the campaigning season of that year as little more than a disaster waiting to happen. Under Marius, the legion gained the mobility, independence, staying power, and readiness that had been lacking or seriously compromised before his logistical reform. Apparently, such disciplinary habits were nothing new, for Polybios (18.18.4–5) mentions legionaries carrying their own *scuta*, *pila*, and sharpened stakes, while Sallust (*B Iug.* 45.2) claims that Marius' predecessor in Numidia, Metellus, had already enforced the practice. Similarly, the use of a wooden dowel in the wooden shaft of the *pilum* (more of which anon) – so that if it stuck in a shield, the dowel would snap and the *pilum* would become an encumbrance – can be seen as a refinement of the long-necked design that went back to the 5th century BC at least, and which was modified further by the introduction of a soft-iron shank in the Caesarian period.

A soldiers' general

Innovator or not, Marius turned out to be an experienced and confident commander who, though lacking the brilliance of Iulius Caesar, understood the basic requirements for a good army were training, discipline, and leadership. When, for instance, he conditioned his army to meet the northern tribes, there were long route marches, each man carrying his gear and preparing his own meals. More a common soldier than an aristocratic

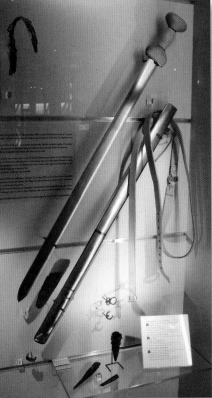

general, Plutarch describes how in Africa Marius had 'won the affection of the soldiers by showing he could live as hard as they did and endure as much' (*Mar.* 7.2). The biographer continues:

> And what a Roman soldier likes most to see is his general eating his rations of common bread with the rest, or sleeping on a simple pallet, or joining in the work of digging a trench or raising a palisade. The commanders whom they admire are not so much those who distribute honours and riches as those who take a share in their hardships and their dangers; they have more affection for those who are willing to join in their work than those who indulge them in going easy.
>
> Plut. *Mar.* 7.3

Marius' worth and authority had been tested in war. From his continuous experience he knew soldiers, and he knew how to get the best out of them. Nevertheless, with the *cohors* of six *centuriae* permanently superseding the *manipulus* of two *centuriae* as the basic tactical unit of the legion, Marius and his officers would have had their hands full devising new cohortal battle drills for the coming conflict with the northern tribes.

As every student of Roman warfare appreciates, much of the success of the legion on the battlefield lay in the legionary's sound knowledge of close-formation fighting: legionaries were trained to fight as a team, to trust each other, and to remain steady under pressure. It was this difference that gave the legion its decisive tactical edge. For the sake of argument, let us assume the following details regarding Marius' cohortal training programme:

Phase A

A *legio* of ten *cohortes* is deployed for battle into the traditional *triplex acies* formation, with four *cohortes* in the front line and three each in the middle and rear lines. In this way, the *cohortes* of a *legio* are always supported by *cohortes* of the same *legio*. Each *cohors* is arranged *centuria* by *centuria*, each of which is deployed four ranks deep. In this formation, the *legio* will advance steadily and soundlessly into the combat zone.

Phase B

Legionaries in the front-line *cohortes* first discharge their light *pila*, followed by their heavy *pila*, the latter some 15m or so from the enemy. If the *pila* do not actually hit the enemy, they will often become embedded in their shields, their barbed points making them difficult to withdraw. Handicapped by a *pilum*, a shield becomes a burden to bear.

Phase C

During the confusion caused by this hail of *pila*, the advancing legionaries rapidly draw their *gladii* and charge at a jog into close contact yelling their war cries. The standard drill is to punch the heavy shield boss in the face of the enemy, and jab the sword's razor-sharp point in his belly (we will return to this standard drill later). On breaking the opposition, legionaries are not supposed to break ranks and pursue. On the contrary, their tactical philosophy is to stand their ground. Meanwhile, if so required, legionaries of the second line *cohortes* wait for the order to move forward to reinforce the fighting line.

In battle, physical endurance is of the utmost importance and all soldiers in close contact with danger become emotionally if not physically exhausted as the battle proceeds. When writing of ancient warfare, du Picq notes the great value of the Roman system was that it kept only those units that were necessary at the point of combat and the rest 'outside of the immediate sphere of moral tension' (2006: p. 64). Emotions, as du Picq understood from first-hand experience, play a central role in combat. Soldiers who encounter combat zones experience intense emotional reactions, both positive (including pride, elation, or exhalation) and negative (such as fear, panic, rage, or ignominy). Du Picq (2006: pp. 94–95) found that the voice of self-preservation raised in fear was the principal emotion in the combat zone.

The legion, organized into separate battle lines, was able to hold one-half to two-thirds of its men outside the combat zone – the zone of demoralization – in which the remaining half or third was engaged. Obviously, the skill of a Roman commander lay not in sharing the dangers with his men but in committing his second and third lines at the right moments. Left too late, the fighting line might buckle and break. Committed too soon, and the value of adding fresh soldiers to the mêlée might be wasted.

Train hard, fight harder

Moving from the advantages to the problems of a soldier's life, there is a typicality of warfare

Full-scale reconstruction of a La Tène *scutum*. This is an oval body shield, which, unlike the Italic version, is flat and not semi-cylindrical. Nailed to the front and running vertically from top to bottom is a wooden spindle boss. This is reinforced with a sheet-metal boss-plate. Normally flat boards of wood, *scuta* were faced with leather to protect against the elements, and against splitting caused by sword blows. Equally, copper alloy or iron binding at head and foot served the same function of warding off blows. (Dorieo/Wikimedia Commons/ CC-BY-SA-3.0)

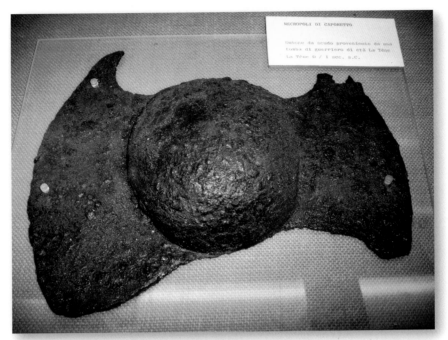

La Tène iron 'butterfly' boss (Trieste, Museo Civico di Storia ed Arte) from the Necropoli di Caporetto, dated to the end of the La Tène period (La Tène D, 150–30 BC). This form, which clearly can be used offensively, is commonly found in middle Europe. (© Esther Carré)

across the ages: mud, rain, cold, baleful heat, suffocating dust, and always a shortage of vittles, along with the ever-present risk of confrontation. Furthermore, geography and distance continue to impose their tyrannies, and obstacles, natural or manmade, suck the momentum out of armies. To be of use, therefore, a fighting army must become the willing instrument of its commander's will. For that reason alone, we may assume that Marius was very much concerned with the proper training and conditioning of his soldiers. It is a military truism that units perform best when they have had an opportunity to train together, develop standard operating procedures, and foster cohesion.

To the daily marches with full equipment and the building (and dismantling) of camps, Marius added training and mock-fighting with weapons, on the model used in gladiatorial school, a method of training (re) introduced in the army by Publius Rutilius Rufus. Finally, by making the eagle (*aquila*) the sole standard of the legion as a whole, Marius improved the unity of the armies and gave the soldiers a symbol that expressed their attachment to an all-encompassing body, an institution to which the soldiers' loyalty could be directed (Plin. 10.4.16). The military reforms made by Marius drastically improved the fighting ability of the Roman military. As we shall see anon, the brutal encounters with the Ambrones and Teutones at Aquae Sextiae, and with the Cimbri at Vercellae the following campaigning season, would provide a sufficiently stern test for the *muli Mariani*.

The forgotten soldier

The development of the army, its recruitment and relations with the political apparatus of the late Republic, is one of the important issues in the history of Rome during the hundred or so years prior to the establishment of the Principate under Augustus. Regrettably, since we have a tendency to concentrate upon Marius and his reforms, one of the architects of this change

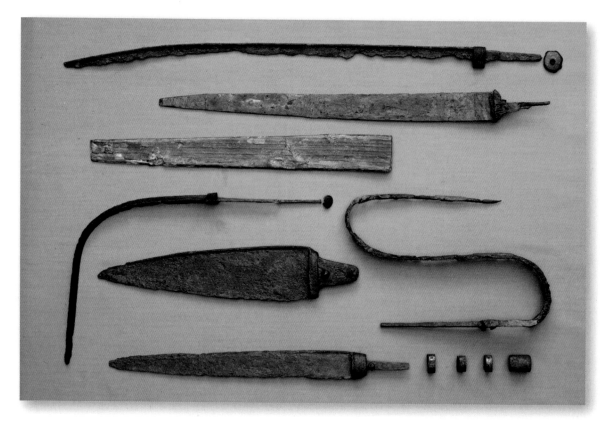

Various swords (København, Nationalmuseet) from the votive deposit at Hjortspring Mose on the island of Als in Sønderjyland, southern Denmark. The Hjortspring deposit contained many items of La Tène B (380–250 BC) war gear, including 131 wooden shields, 33 shield bosses, remains of several mail-shirts (a rare find in northern Iron Age Europe), 138 iron spearheads, and long slashing swords (two deliberately bent), along with a clinker-built boat of knot-free linden measuring more than 19m in length overall. The whole assemblage was placed in a tiny peat bog around 350 BC (Randsborg 1999: pp. 192–98). This was probably a gift to the gods following a victory over a seaborne incursion. Deposits in bogs and pools are prominent elements in cult practice in northern Europe from the later Neolithic onwards, with the largest and best-known in Denmark. (Lennart Larsen/Wikimedia Commons/CC-BY-SA-3.0)

tends to be reduced to a passing mention, a footnote if not totally neglected. Briefly, here is his story.

Publius Rutilius Rufus (b. 158 BC) was the great-uncle of Iulius Caesar (through his sister Rutilia, Caesar's maternal grandmother) and the fellow consul of Cnaeus Mallius Maximus in 105 BC (more of him anon). Well-known as a Stoic philosopher, Rutilius was very much interested in the science of warfare, and in his lifetime he was to gain a well-deserved reputation as a military theorist and author. For instance, the first-rate narration of the engagement at the Muthul River strongly suggests Sallust (*B Iug.* 48–53) used Rutilius as his primary source here – Rutilius was present at the battle as a *legatus* under Metellus (ibid. 50.1) – though sadly for us his *commentarii* have been extinguished by the malevolence of time. Of course, it should not be forgotten that Rutilius was not only a thinker, but had seen plenty of service in the field, too.

Scipio Aemilianus had picked Rutilius to join his staff (*consilium*) in the expedition against Numantia (Cic. *Rep.* 1.17, App. *Iber.* 14.88). On that gruelling campaign (as we have already noted), he served alongside future greats like Marius, Caius Gracchus, and the Numidian prince Iugurtha, who was still an ally of Rome at the time (App. *Iber.* 14.88). Caius Memmius (*tr. pl.* 111 BC) was also there (Frontin. 4.1.1), and, perhaps, the future *princeps senatus* Marcus Aemilius Scaurus (*cos.* 115 BC, *cen.* 109 BC), too (*Vir. ill.* 72.3).

Rutilius made *praetor* in 118 BC, which meant he could legally seek the consulship three years after that. The cunning and crooked Scaurus, a steady supporter of the newly ascendant Caecilii Metelli, would be a bitter rival at the elections for 115 BC (with reciprocal allegations of *ambitus*), and Rutilius would not reach the consulship until a decade had elapsed.

Before then, Rutilius would join the honest Quintus Metellus as a *legatus* in the war against Iugurtha, now king of the Numidians (109 BC). Two years later, when Metellus left in a huff before Marius could take over the command of the Numidian war, Rutilius had the dubious honour of handing Marius the keys (Sall. *B Iug.* 86.4–5, Plut. *Mar.* 10.1). Rutilius was to become a personal foe and committed political opponent of Marius.

Rutilius was elected to the consulship in 105 BC, at an age above 50. This, of course, was the very year that witnessed the catastrophic clash at Arausio. For some unexplained reason, however, Rutilius was not appointed to take charge of the military campaign against the northern tribes. As an experienced soldier and veteran of the recent war in Numidia – he had greatly distinguished himself in the battle of the Muthul – this does appear to be a genuine catastrophic blunder on the Senate's part. As it turned out, Rutilius remained in Rome while his junior and less-experienced colleague, Cnaeus Mallius Maximus, marched north with his consular army.

While in Rome, Rutilius was to introduce the methods of the gladiatorial schools into military training. Having raised his two consular legions, Rutilius then hired gladiatorial trainers (*doctoribus gladiatorum*) from the school of Caius Aurelius Scaurus to demonstrate to his soldiers how to duck and parry better (Val. Max. 2.3.2).[4] We can safely assume that these men were expert technicians with vast experience and deep knowledge of weapon handling. The following year, while he was busy making preparations for the war against the Cimbri and Teutones, Marius was so impressed by the soldiers trained under Rutilius that he preferred them to his own African veterans, choosing 'the army of Rutilius, though it was the smaller of the two, because he thought it was the better trained and disciplined' (Frontin. 4.2.2). Perhaps we should be crediting Rutilius with training the army that went on to defeat the northern tribes.

Unlucky to the end, Rutilius would succumb to a malicious prosecution in 92 BC, and he would be forced into exile by a kangaroo court. Ironically, this would be spent in the province of Asia among the very Greeks he was alleged to have defrauded two years earlier. Here, in Smyrna, he would find friendship and solace in discussing philosophy and writing his *commentarii* as well as a history of Rome in Greek (Vell. 2.13.2). The dictator Sulla invited him to return to Rome, but Rutilius refused to do so. In 78 BC, towards the very end of his life, Rutilius would be paid a visit by an up-and-coming young lawyer, a certain Cicero.

In his youth, Rutilius had studied philosophy under the intellectual and moral colossus Panaitios of Rhodes (b. *c.* 185 BC), who spent a considerable amount of time in Rome and in the circle of Scipio Aemilianus. It was this great Stoic who once wrote, 'The life of men who pass their time in the midst of affairs, and who wish to be helpful to themselves and to others, is exposed to constant and almost daily troubles and sudden dangers' (fr. 8 apud Gell. 13.28). Though he was not speaking of his former student, he might as well have been.

---

4   The elder Cato (*De re militari* fr. 14) also mentions gladiatorial training, so Rutilius Rufus may not have been the first to introduce such methods into the Roman army.

Migratory routes of the Cimbri and Teutones

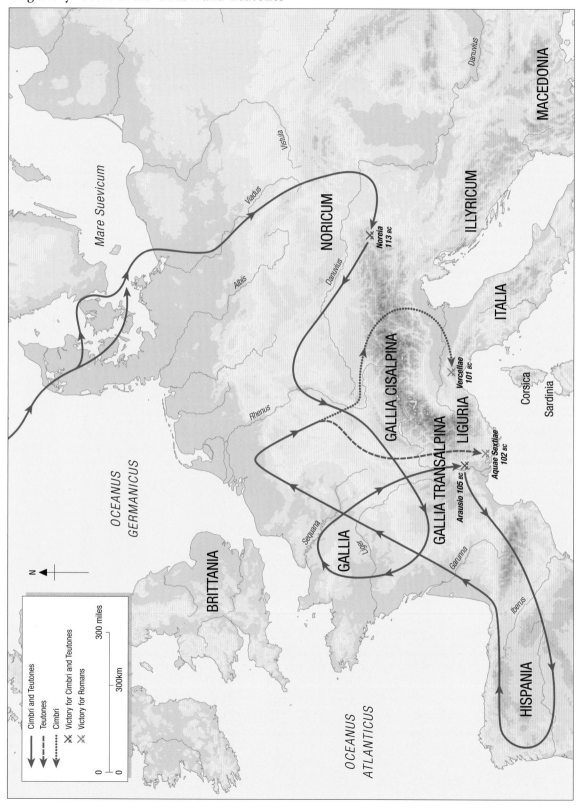

THE CIMBRIAN WAR

FIRST ENCOUNTERS, 113–107 BC

> Neither Samnite nor Carthaginian, neither Hispania nor Gaul, nor even the Parthians has taught us more lessons. The Germani fighting for liberty has been a keener enemy than the absolutism of Arsaces.
>
> Tacitus *Germania* 37.3–4

When Tacitus wrote down these words, the Cimbri, 'a name mighty in history' (*Germ.* 37.1), were a spent tribal force. Some 210 years previously, by Tacitus' reckoning, the Cimbri (and the Teutones) quit their northern homeland, and headed south-east across central Europe. Having ventured into the Balkan peninsula, however, they were driven back by the Scordisci. It was at this point that the two tribes about-faced and headed west, bringing a major threat to the northern fringes of the Roman world.

In 113 BC, the migrants encountered the Taurisci in what was then known as Noricum (centred on what is now Austria and north-eastern Italy). A confederation of Celtic tribes, the Taurisci were *socius et amicus Romani populi* ('ally and friend of the Roman people'), and sent emissaries to the Senate seeking help in dealing with what was an overwhelming threat. Rome had always been fixated with tribal movements, and the consul Cnaeus Papirius Carbo was sent across the Alpes Iulii (Julian Alps) to deal with the situation at the head of some 30,000 troops. Hearing rumours of the military might of the Republic, even if they were strangers to Rome, the two tribes accepted Carbo's proposal to pull back away from the Italian peninsula. He then offered guides to escort them out of the territory of the Taurisci. But it was a ruse.

Not content with a peaceful resolution, Carbo wanted the triumph that he hoped a victory would crown him with. He was counting on a surprise attack. The guides were instructed to lead the tribes towards Noreia, where the consul would set an ambush. Strabo (5.1.8) vaguely locates Noreia somewhere in the mountain country north-east of Aquileia, while Livy just has 'the Cimbri came to Illyricum' (*Per.* 63.5), which basically implies the precise location was unknown, and it was already referred to by Pliny (3.19 §131) as lost to history. As for the gauntlet of ambush, it did not turn out that way.

Full-sized manikin (Požarevac Narodni muzej) representing a Scordisci warrior. He is depicted with typical La Tène war gear discovered through archaeological digs: long slashing sword, broad-bladed spearhead, and iron shield boss. The Scordisci were a Celtic group formed after the Gallic invasion of the Balkans who heavily mixed with the local Thracians and Illyrians. The Scordisci were strong enough to deflect the Cimbri and Teutones westwards, and a couple of years later a Roman army in Macedonia, under Caius Porcius Cato (*cos.* 114 BC), would be ignominiously routed by the same peoples. (Isidora Lazović/Wikimedia Commons/ CC-BY-SA-4.0)

For some unexplained reason, the Cimbri managed to discover the consul's plot and turned the tables on the Romans. The ambushers became the ambushed and walked straight into ruin. Without warning, the Cimbri swiftly smashed full force into the Roman column-of-march, swinging and slashing and cutting and chopping their way amongst the surprised Roman soldiers. Under this unexpected, brutally swift onslaught they crumbled within minutes. The Roman army no longer existed, its former presence confirmed by scattered survivors seeking safety, and pierced, mutilated, and bloodied bodies lying in attitudes of defence or escape. It is reported only about 6,000 Romans managed to escape, the triumph-seeking Carbo among their number. In less time than a written account of it takes to read, the Cimbri had made short work of the consular army.

Carbo violated one of war's time-honoured principles: underestimating his enemy while overestimating his own capabilities. This boiled down to the same thing: he let *hubris* get the better of him. And so it was that Carbo fell victim to the vengeance of Nemesis and was denied the triumph he so earnestly desired. On this matter Appianus pulls no punches when he says:

[Carbo] suffered for his perfidy, and lost a large part of his army. He would probably have perished with his whole force had not darkness and a tremendous thunderstorm fallen upon them while the fight was in progress, separating the combatants and putting an end to the battle by sheer terror from heaven.

App. *Kelt*. fr. 13

A re-enactor equipped as an aristocratic Gaulish warrior. He wears a mail-shirt with shoulder reinforcements modelled after those of the Greek *linothōrax*. Observe the position of his right hand as he prepares to draw his long slashing sword: having inverted the hand to grasp the hilt, he will now push the pommel forward so as to draw the sword with no difficulty. (Metelos/Wikimedia Commons/CC-BY-SA-3.0)

Thus, fortunately for the surviving Romans, torrential rain stopped play; if not, the backlash would have been more brutal. Iulius Obsequens, the late-antique portent collector, while diligently recording his prodigies for that year recounts that, 'After crossing the Alps, the Cimbri and Teutones cruelly slaughtered the Romans and their allies' (38). Carbo was indicted for losing his army, but escaped conviction by committing suicide.

Silver drachma *à la tête cubiste* (Paris, BNP Cabinet des Médailles) of the Volcae Tectosages, dated 121–52 BC. On the obverse is a male head in 'cubist' style, while the reverse exhibits an axe on the lower left. (PHGCOM/Wikimedia Commons/CC-BY-SA-3.0)

Many a victory has been robbed of its fruits by the victor's obvious inability to exploit his success. On this particular occasion, the Cimbri and Teutones might well have pushed southwards into the Italian peninsula without resistance, but instead moved westwards to the upper Rhenus (Rhine) River and into Gaul, leaving chaos in their wake. Following Carbo's shambolic campaign, which had ended in a shameful rout, another tribe, the Tigurini (one of the tribal groupings of the Helvetii), joined the Cimbri–Teutones alliance and ventured westwards into Gaul with them. In 109 BC, the three tribes circled back from their excursion in Gaul.

General view of the Garonne valley as seen from Saint-Émilion. It was somewhere in this river basin en route to Burdigala (Bordeaux) that Marius' colleague in the consulship of 107 BC, Lucius Cassius Longinus, was ambushed and killed by the Tigurini. In an act of complete humiliation, the surviving Roman soldiers were forced to pass under the yoke.
(© Esther Carré)

Near the frontier of Gallia Transalpina, only recently annexed and established as a Roman *provincia*, the three tribes came up against a consular army led by the consul Marcus Iunius Silanus (Liv. *Per*. 65.2). Doubting the outcome of battle, they offered to serve Rome in return for land on the frontier of the province, sending envoys to the camp of Silanus proposing that 'the people of Mars should give them some land by way of pay and use their hands and weapons for any purpose they wished' (Flor. 1.38.2). The Senate, the initiating body of war and peace, was to make the same mistake again: so much for learning from the past. Chauvinistic contempt for their opponents convinced the senators that the three tribes lacked the will to fight back, and so they declined the offer.

Fierce, unforgiving opponents, the three tribes cut to pieces the consular army of Silanus, but, as with the case of Carbo four years earlier, the victors did not follow up their advantage. The Cimbri and Teutones continued westwards through Gaul, while the Tigurini broke off to raid Gallia Transalpina, provoking a revolt of the Volcae Tectosages, a Celtic tribe subject to Rome (Dio 27 F90.1). Like Carbo, Silanus was indicted for losing his army, the charge being that he had engaged with the Northerners, '*iniussi populi*' (Ascon. 80C).

In 107 BC, Marius' colleague in the consulship, Lucius Cassius Longinus, advanced to redeem the calamity that had befallen Roman arms. At first, all went well for Longinus. Just outside Tolosa (Toulouse), the two armies met, and, despite the disparity in numbers, the Romans were victorious. The Tigurini retreated in disorder, leaving behind their baggage wagons. Flushed with success, Longinus followed the Tigurini towards the Iberian frontier, but he did not want to leave behind the captured baggage train, which impeded the movement of his army. He was defeated and killed in an ambush 'in the territory of the Nitiobriges' (Liv. *Per*. 65.5, cf. Caes. *B Gall*. 7.7.2), which was somewhere in the Guranna (Garonne) valley south-east of Burdigala (Bordeaux).

The survivors under the dead consul's *legatus* (Caius Popillius Laenas), having been surrounded and left with no way of escape, were permitted to

A *vomitorium* at the Roman amphitheatre in Toulouse (ancient Tolosa), built during the reign of Claudius (AD 41–54). Tolosa was the chief *civitas* of the Volcae Tectosages, Celts who joined the Germanic Cimbri and Teutones when they arrived in southern Gaul. Tolosa was sacked in retribution by Quintus Servilius Caepio, who apparently helped himself to the legendary *aurum Tolosanum*, part of the plunder taken during the Gaulish sack of Delphi in 279 BC. Subsequently, Tolosa and its hinterland were integrated into Gallia Transalpina. (© Esther Carré)

withdraw after being 'made to pass under the yoke' (Caes. *B. Gall.* 1.7.3). This was a complete and utter humiliation. The yoke was made of two spears fixed upright, with a third fastened horizontally across them at such a height that the defeated and stripped soldiers filing under it were obliged to stoop in token of submission. It must have been doubly galling that the Tigurini had chosen this gesture, since it was an ancient Italic custom, and, as is well known, an indignity the Romans had suffered once before at the Caudine Forks in 321 BC. Caius Popillius 'was eventually charged with treason' (Anon. *ad Herennium* 1.25).

Rome was now desperate for a victory. In 106 BC, the consul Quintus Servilius Caepio managed to subdue the Volcae Tectosages, who had recently turned against Rome, and seized their chief *civitas* of Tolosa, though he could achieve little else. However, it was rumoured that the consul had stolen a sizeable fortune in gold when he took Tolosa. Orosius tells us that:

> After capturing a Gallic town called Tolosa the proconsul [*sic*] Caepio removed 100,000 pounds [32,890kg] of gold and 110,000 pounds [36,180kg] of silver from the temple of Apollo. After it had been sent under guard to Massilia, all of it is said to have been criminally made away with. This led in due course to a large-scale inquiry at Rome.

> Oros. 5.15.25

Strabo (4.1.13), quoting Poseidonios,[5] puts the combined value of the gold and silver bullion at around 15,000 talents, which is either some 390,000kg (Attic standard) or 480,000kg (Roman standard). Whatever the true weight of this hoarded fortune, Justinus says 'all the gold and silver from Tolosa was stolen by the Roman consul Caepio' (32.3.10). According to legend, this treasure was first stolen from the temple of Apollo at Delphi by the Scordisci during the Gallic invasion of the Balkan peninsula in 279 BC (Dio 27 F90.1). The inquiry mentioned by Orosius was ultimately held in Rome in 104 BC before a special court. We have no record of the outcome, but apparently, Lucius Appuleius Saturninus (more on him later) had plans to use the stolen treasure to fund the settlement of Marius' veterans (*Vir. ill.* 73.5).

The theft of the gold was soon overshadowed by the debacle at Arausio, resulting in Caepio being stripped of his offices and citizenship, fined 15,000 talents, and losing his property (Just. 32.3.10, Dio 27 F90.1). Dispatched into well-deserved exile, he ended his days living at ease in Smyrna (Livy *Per.* 67.3, Ascon. 78C, Val. Max. 4.7.3). His granddaughter was Servilia, mistress of Iulius Caesar and mother of Marcus Iunius Brutus, leader of Caesar's assassins. The *aurum Tolosanum* was never found, and was rumoured to have been handed all the way down to the last heir of the Servilii Caepiones, Marcus

---

5 Poseidonios of Apameia is widely regarded as the most fully informed on the peoples encountered by Rome in Western Europe. He was a Syrian Greek who studied in Athens, embraced Stoic philosophy, and wrote on a huge number of subjects between about 110 BC and 50 BC. Most of this vast corpus is lost, but surviving fragments attest to his deep interest in ethnology. He may have been the first Graeco-Roman writer to make a clear distinction between the Celts and Germani.

Brutus, who was to take his own life after the decisive battle of Philippi in 42 BC. The sources make frequent allusions to the gold being cursed, with Justinus suggesting that the 'rising of the Cimbrian War ... seemed to pursue the Romans as if to avenge the removal of that devoted treasure' (32.3.11).

ARAUSIO, 105 BC

Aurum habet Tolosanum / He has got the gold of Tolosa

Latin proverb

What of the Cimbri and the Teutones in all this? Despite tribal armies being frequently sizeable, but invariably clumsy in their movements, for a number of years the two tribes disappear from the written record. We next hear of them when they sent emissaries to the Senate in Rome requesting land along the Rhenus (Rhine) River. The request was denied. In 105 BC, a Cimbrian host moved down the east bank of the Rhodanus (Rhône) River to Arausio (Orange), currently the furthest Roman outpost in Gallia Transalpina. Waiting for them was the consul Cnaeus Mallius Maximus and Quintus Servilius Caepio (*cos.* 106 BC), now proconsul of Gallia Cisalpina after the expiration of his consulship. Together they commanded two consular armies: each would have consisted of two legions and of twice as many allies, totalling around 60,000 men at the very most. 'It was one day before the nones of October' (Plut. *Lucull.* 27.7)[6] that two uncoordinated engagements were to be played out on the left bank of the broad and swift-moving Rhodanus. The stage was set for a Roman calamity.

The disaster
Truth be told, none of this was necessary. Yet owing to bickering between the two commanders – a pitched battle promised booty and a chance for glory and a triumph perhaps, but for one not two – the Romans blew it. Although consul Mallius was technically the superior commander, as a *novus homo* he was looked down upon by the socially superior Caepio. Initially, the two commanders took up separate positions on either bank of the Rhodanus, Caepio on the right bank, Mallius on the left, near the settlement of Arausio. When it became clear that the enemy was closing in on Mallius' position, Caepio began to worry that his rival would gain sole credit for the forthcoming victory over the barbarians. He therefore crossed the river, although he still refused to establish a common camp with Mallius (Dio 27.91.1). The entreaties of his soldiers finally induced him to confer with his superior commander. In spite of this, due to mutual jealousy and dislike between the pair, the interview ended badly, with Caepio refusing to partake in Mallius' plan of action against the northern tribes (ibid. 91.3). On top of this, Mallius appears to have failed to maintain tight discipline in his camp.

The end result, in retrospect, was entirely predictable: the two consular armies were pushed back against the Rhodanus, first Caepio's and then Mallius', where they were pinned and ripped to pieces in turn. Livy (*Per.* 67.2, quoting Valerius Antias) claims all 80,000 troops died on the field, while 40,000 servants and camp followers were slaughtered in the immediate

---

6   The nones of October fell on the 7th, placing the battle on 6 October 105 BC.

The battle of Arausio, 6 October 105 BC

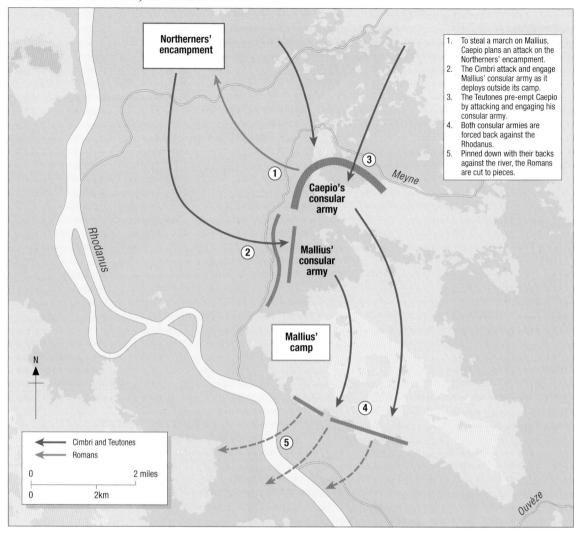

Northerners' encampment

1. To steal a march on Mallius, Caepio plans an attack on the Northerners' encampment.
2. The Cimbri attack and engage Mallius' consular army as it deploys outside its camp.
3. The Teutones pre-empt Caepio by attacking and engaging his consular army.
4. Both consular armies are forced back against the Rhodanus.
5. Pinned down with their backs against the river, the Romans are cut to pieces.

Meyne

Caepio's consular army

Rhodanus

Mallius' consular army

Mallius' camp

N

Cimbri and Teutones
Romans

0   2 miles
0   2km

Ouvèze

aftermath. Only ten men were reputed to have avoided death that day (Oros. 5.16.4). Though all this is undoubtedly an exaggeration – Diodorus Siculus (36.8.1) is content with 66,000 dead – the double defeat on the plain near Arausio was prodigious, one whose scale and horror destroyed the Romans in a disaster of their own making.

Among those lucky few to escape the carnage were Mallius (who lost his two sons that day) and Caepio, as well as one of Caepio's *contubernales* by the name of Quintus Sertorius, destined to be an implacable foe of Sulla's. Having lost his horse and 'wounded in many parts of his body', in his moment of need Sertorius plunged into the broad and swift-flowing river, 'swimming, shield and breastplate and all, against a strongly adverse current' (Plut. *Sert.* 3.1), and safely made it to the right bank. Sertorius was to take great pride in his war wounds, all frontal and including a gouged-out eye (Sall. *Hist.* 1 fr. 76 Ramsey). Such heroics aside, and no matter the exact butcher's bill, the consular armies of Mallius and Caepio had not survived: they had been smashed.

A grisly end

Caepio's arrogance and lust for glory had led to a colossal defeat at the hands of the northern tribes. But for those who managed to survive the trouncing but failed to flee the killing field, the worst was yet to come. Orosius mentions the sacrifice of Roman prisoners by the Cimbri, along with the spoils taken from the two Roman camps:

> Having gained possession of both camps and of a huge amount of booty, the enemy by some strange and unusual curse completely destroyed everything they captured; clothing was cut to pieces and strewn about, gold and silver were thrown into the [Rhodanus] river, the breastplates of men were hacked to pieces, the trappings of the horses were ruined, the horses themselves were drowned in whirlpools, and men, with nooses around their necks, hanged from trees. Thus the conqueror realized no booty, while the conquered obtained no mercy.
>
> Oros. 5.16.5–6

There was a widespread belief among the Germani (and Celts) that wet locations were sacred places where you could contact the gods. Of the bodies recovered from pools and bogs, a high proportion of them have clearly died in violent circumstances, by strangulation, stabbing, lynching, decapitation, and drowning. Some were immersed naked, others clothed. The Rhodanus that day must have been stuffed with the corpses of Romans, some of which would have been maimed before being sent to their watery grave, briefly bobbing above the surface before vanishing into the gulping river.

Human sacrifice is amply attested to in the archaeological record. Hundreds of bodies, some astonishingly well preserved, have been recovered from pools and peat bogs in northern Germany and southern Scandinavia, often ritually drowned or decapitated. Tacitus, it must be noted, is remarkably even-handed when he comes to discuss the cultic traditions of the Germani, giving them credit for piety, respect of tradition, devotion to divination, and absence of anthropomorphism. One such Germanic tradition, as Tacitus

Arc de triomphe, Orange. This triumphal arch spanned the Via Agrippa on its approach to the city. It was erected to honour veterans of the Gallic Wars and, in particular, *legio* II *Gallica* (later *Augusta*: *vide* Capricorn emblem, birth sign of Octavianus, on officer's shield, left north façade), veterans of which founded Roman Arausio in or after 35 BC (*CIL* XII 3203). Current consensus dates the monumental arch to the reign of Augustus (27 BC–AD 14). Celtic Arausio lay on the fertile plain on the left bank of the Rhodanus, and close by was the spot where two consular armies were crushed on the same day by the Cimbri and Teutones. (Donarreiskoffer/Wikimedia Commons/CC-BY-SA-4.0)

ANNIHILATION AT ARAUSIO, 6 OCTOBER 105 BC (PP. 54–55)

Early Iron Age Germanic society was a warrior society, one geared to waging war – within tribes, between different peoples, and against external enemies. Despite the customary ethnic stereotyping (tall of stature, red-gold hair, fierce blue eyes, lacking stamina, etc.), Tacitus still remains our best literary source for the tactical methods employed by the Germani. On this particular subject, he is worth quoting in full:

Few have swords or the longer kind of spear: they carry short spears, in their language *frameae*, with a narrow and small iron head, so sharp and so handy in use they fight with the same weapon, as circumstances demand, both at close quarters and at a distance. The horse warrior is content with *frameae* and shield: the foot warriors launch showers of missiles in addition, each man a volley, and hurl these to great distances, for they wear no outer clothing, or at most a cloak. There is no bravery of apparel among them: their shields only are picked out with choice colours. Few have body armour: scarcely one or two at most have metal or rawhide helmets. Their horses are conspicuous neither for beauty nor speed; but then neither are they trained like our horses to run in shifting circles: they ride them forwards only or to wheel to the right in a compact body so that none is left behind.

Tac. Germ. 6.1–3, cf. Ann. 2.14

Horses were small: this and the nature of the terrain in Germania accounted for the fact that warriors were often at their most effective – not to mention safest – when firmly planting their feet on the ground rather than precariously seated on horseback. Finds of Germanic weaponry in graves and votive deposits, and bronze statuettes and sculpted scenes of combat involving Germani on bas-reliefs of the Principate, present the same general picture.

In this reconstruction, the Cimbri and the Teutones (**1**) have successfully rolled over the two consular armies (**2**, note, these were still made up of manipular legions). With little likelihood of escape, the survivors are being driven back towards the fast-flowing Rhodanus. Though the two consular commanders have made good their escape across to the right bank of the river, one of Caepio's young staff officers, Quintus Sertorius (**3**), is attempting to stem the tide and offer some resistance with those men still courageous enough to stand and fight the oncoming Germani. He has been joined by a couple of hard-bitten centurions (**4**). Their chances of success, of course, are slim to nil.

records, was that which 'cowards, shirkers, sodomites are pressed down under a wicker hurdle into the slimy mud of a bog' (*Germ.* 12.1). Those powerful lines of Matthew Arnold come to mind: 'Cowards, who were in sloughs interr'd alive; / And round them still the wattle hurdles hung / Wherewith they stamp'd them down, and trod them deep, / To hide their shameful memory from men' (*Balder Dead*, 'Journey to the Dead').

The utter distaste of Graeco-Roman authors for human sacrifice is evident from their writings, invariably describing it as a 'monster-revealing mirror' that exposes the true nature of the northern peoples. Strabo, writing a century before Tacitus, dwells on the practice of human sacrifice by the Cimbri. White-clad, grey-haired priestesses accompanying the warriors supervised the sacrifice of selected prisoners of war by suspending them over great bronze cauldrons (each capable of holding 20 *amphorae*, or 524 litres) and cutting their throats, so that their lifeblood flowed down into vessels below. Some priestesses would observe each victim's blood for divinatory purposes, 'while still others would split open the body and from an inspection of the entrails would utter a prophecy of victory for their own people' (Strab. 7.2.3).

Meanwhile in Rome

Even for militaries with extensive experience, war remains a difficult business. For Rome at this juncture, the war against the northern tribes had reached a ghastly crescendo. Unsurprisingly, therefore, the terrible news of Arausio triggered a major stir in the bustling metropolis, a panic even (Oros. 5.16.7). This was so much so that for the very last time in their history the Romans performed a human sacrifice, burying alive two men and two women, Greek and Gaulish, in the Forum Boarium (Plut. *Mor.* 283F–284C, cf. Liv. 22.57.6). As Caesar was to artfully remind them a half century hence, the Romans were always sensitive to any tribal threats from the north, having long memories of the sack of Rome by the Gauls. The Italic peninsula was now open to invasion, and nothing stood between Rome and the two tribes but a surprising decision on their part. Would the year 104 BC turn out to be a horrifying sequel to 105 BC?

Instead of turning east to cross the Alps, the Cimbri and Teutones parted ways. The Cimbri then crossed the Pyrenees into the Iberian peninsula and remained there for the next three years, their southern sojourn being terminated after suffering a crushing defeat at the hands of the Celtiberians. 'They returned to Gaul to rejoin the Teutones in the land of the Veliocasses'

Town of Fos-sur-mer (*Fòs de mar* in Provençal), *département* of Bouches-du-Rhône, viewed from the ramparts of the old town. The *Fossæ Marianæ*, literary 'trench of Marius', was a canal dug by Marius' soldiers from the Rhodanus to the Mediterranean near Fos-sur-mer (Plut. *Mar.* 15.1–4). It was constructed to avoid the difficult navigation at the mouths of the river, caused by the accumulation of silt by several watercourses (Strab. 1.4.8), so solving Marius' logistical problems. The canal was some 17.5 Roman miles (25.75km) long. After the campaign against the Teutones and Ambrones, Marius gave the canal to the Massiliotes as a reward for their recent aid. A 5km stretch of the canal was confirmed by an excavation in 2013 and geophysical surveys the following year. At the north, the canal section terminates in the Grand-Rhône leading to Arles (Arelate). At the south, the canal section is lost in the wetlands. (Malost/Wikimedia Commons/CC-BY-SA-3.0)

(Liv. *Per.* 67.8, cf. Oros. 6.7.14), a Belgic peoples dwelling near the mouth of the Sequana (Seine) River. In the meantime, the Teutones had wandered through northern and western Gaul. Italy had been spared what would no doubt have been a major invasion akin to that mounted by the Celtic Senones in 390 BC when they routed the Romans at the Allia River and briefly occupied and sacked Rome itself, all save the Capitol. The controversy surrounding the reasons for this disaster at Arausio undoubtedly buzzed in every ear in Rome. Worse still, this was the latest in a series of spectacular defeats inflicted upon Roman armies by the northern tribes. The northern menace now became Marius' next concern.

In the autumn of 105 BC, a pro-Marian lobby secured for Marius a second consulship. This was technically illegal, since Marius was not even in Rome for the election – he was currently in Numidia winding up the war with its king, Iugurtha. But it was not without precedent, as Scipio Aemilianus had been elected consul while absent from Rome (Cic. *Rep.* 6.11). On the other hand, its acquisition within a decade of his first was both theoretically unconstitutional and illegal, though Livy (7.42.2, 10.13.8) states plainly that no law was sacrosanct. Indeed, it does appear that Marius had the backing of the Senate, as Gallia Transalpina was allotted to him as his consular province (Sall. *B Iug.* 114.3, Vell. 2.12.1, Liv. *Per.* 67.5). Fifty years later, Cicero would pose the following rhetorical question in the Senate:

> Who had more personal enemies than Caius Marius? Lucius [Licinius] Crassus and Marcus [Aemilius] Scaurus disliked him, all the [Caecilii] Metelli hated him. Yet so far from voting against the grant of the province of Gallia Transalpina to their enemy, these men supported the extraordinary command of that province to him so that he might command in the war against the Gauls [i.e. Cimbri and Teutones].
>
> Cic. *Prov. cons.* 19

Though Marius held up for the *nobilitas* a mirror in which they saw reflected their own incompetence, his most powerful *inimici* in the Senate did nothing to counter Marius being assigned Gallia Transalpina as his consular province so he could pursue the Cimbrian War. Such was the fear of the possibility of the northern tribes descending upon Italy.

What is more, violating precedent, Marius was to be elected consul a further four times (103–100 BC, *cos.* III–VI), thus giving him six consulships to date. There are other examples of Roman generals retaining command of an army during a period of *tumultus*: Quintus Fabius Maximus Cunctator during the initial years of the war with Hannibal, for instance. The vital difference, however, lies in the fact that when the year of consulship ended, these commanders were given proconsular rank. There was no precedent for Marius' string of back-to-back consulships, an offence to the idea of limited tenure of office. For Marius, however, the days when he could sit back and tell himself, sure in the knowledge of victory, what a fine job he had done, were a long way off.

It is deeply ironic that, in its own way, the horrendous slaughter at Arausio hastened the demise of the Republic, as it permitted unprecedented power to accumulate in the hands of one man. Later on, Marius, having reached the cusp of power and prestige, would wield that power and prestige against Rome itself. What is more, at the end of the Cimbrian War the ambitious Marius bestowed Roman citizenship on a number of his Italian soldiers in clear defiance of the Senate, thus setting another dangerous precedent. Far more importantly, however, was that the military reforms of Marius were to eventually lead to a more professional, long-service army, which would increasingly express its loyalty to its generals rather than to the Senate. And so the Republic had taken a path of no return, one which had the footprint of civil strife left by Marius. The inner wisdom of the Ephesian philosopher Herakleitos scores again: 'War is father of all, king of all' (fr. B 53 Diels-Kranz).

Panoramic view of Arles (Arelate), *département* of Bouches-du-Rhône, looking southwards towards the Camargue. The strategic importance of Arelate for the Romans lay in its location at the lowest bridging point of the Rhodanus (Rhône) River. Moreover, a few kilometres downstream sat the head of the Rhodanus (Camargue) delta, and the city was also the point where the river forked into two main branches. The Romans took the settlement from the Ligurians in 123 BC. Marius' army camped here during their construction of the *Fossæ Marianæ*. (Chensiyuan/ Wikimedia Commons/ CC-BY-SA-4.0)

AQUAE SEXTIAE, 102 BC

Teutoni a Mario traucidati / The Teutones were slaughtered by Marius

Iulius Obsequens 44

Safely back in Rome and presumably having recovered from his war wounds, Quintus Sertorius joined Marius, almost certainly as a member of his *consilium*. When the Cimbri moved away from the Roman frontier, Sertorius followed them, apparently disguised as a Celt, keeping Marius informed of their activities (Plut. *Sert.* 3.2). This story may or may not be true, but commanders throughout history have, each in his day, devoted much of their time to outguessing and outwitting their foes by acquiring as accurate a picture as possible of their intentions, capabilities, and strength. The Duke of Wellington expressed this major mental effort very succinctly as, 'guessing what was at the other side of the hill'.[7] 'The other side of the hill' was to Marius, encamped in Gallia Transalpina, the land beyond the Roman frontier, and somewhere out there were roaming the northern tribes. Marius needed first-hand military intelligence so as to keep abreast of their activities.

Waiting for the barbarians

One of the universal principles of war is surprise. As a general, Marius relied mainly on surprise and always showed a reluctance to engage in a traditional, set-piece fight. Made of less spectacular stuff than his nephew Caesar would turn out to be, Marius preferred to determine the time and place, and would not be hurried. Such was to be his victory at Aquae Sextiae.

Marius' consular colleague, Quintus Lutatius Catulus, was sent north to hold the Alpine passes against the Cimbri and the Tigurini, who were

---

7 Statement in conversation with John Wilson Croker (4 September 1852), as quoted in *The Croker Papers* (London, 1884), vol. 3, p. 276.

Confluence of the Isère (left) and the Rhône (right) near the commune of Le Roche-de-Glun, *département* of Drôme. It was in the vicinity of the confluence of the two rivers that Marius' army first encountered the Teutones and the Ambrones. According to Plutarch (*Mar.* 18.1–2), it took six days for the Northerners to pass Marius' fortified camp; as they passed, they mockingly asked the Romans hunkered down within for messages to pass on to their wives and daughters in Rome. (Mrfido/Wikimedia Commons/CC0 1.0)

currently somewhere in Noricum. Meanwhile, Marius crossed over into Gallia Transalpina, where he was to first encounter the Teutones and Ambrones 'near the confluence of the Rhodanus [Rhône] and the Isara [Isère] rivers' (Oros. 5.16.9, cf. Strab. 4.1.8, Polyb. 3.49.5, Liv. 21.31.4). It was here that Marius 'built a fortified camp along the Rhodanus' (Plut. *Mar.* 15.1), which was providential as this first sighting of the northern tribes caused some consternation in the rank and file of Marius' army. In the words of Plutarch:

> Their numbers were limitless, they were hideous in their aspect, and their speech and cries were unlike those of other people. They covered a large part of the plain, and after pitching their camp challenged Marius to battle. Marius, however, paid no heed to them, but kept his soldiers inside their fortifications, bitterly rebuking those who would have made a display of their courage, and calling those whose high spirit made them wish to rush forth and give battle traitors to their country.
>
> Plut. *Mar.* 15.5–16.1

According to Frontinus, a warrior of the Teutones personally challenged Marius to mortal combat. 'Marius answered that, if the man was desirous of death, he should end his life with a halter.' Then, when the warrior persisted, Marius mocked him by offering him a gladiator whose glory days had long passed, explaining that 'if he would first defeat this gladiator, he himself would then fight with him' (Frontin. 4.7.5).

When Marius did not offer battle, the Teutones and Ambrones attempted to storm the Roman camp. For three days they tired every means 'to dislodge the Romans from their ramparts and drive them out on level ground' (Oros. 5.16.9, cf. Liv. *Per.* 68.2, Plut. *Mar.* 18.1). Failing to make any headway, the Teutones and Ambrones broke camp, crossed the Rhodanus, and moved as a vast mass south-eastwards with the intention of heading for the Italian peninsula. Later commentators saw the wisdom of Marius' judgement in deliberately avoiding action. Niccolò Machiavelli, for one, praised Marius for:

Mount Sainte-Victoire, looking east from Aix-en-Provence, *département* of Bouches-du-Rhône. In this photograph we see two of the four major peaks of the white limestone massif, Croix de Provence (elev. 946m) and Le Signal (elev. 969m). An iconic landmark in Provence, the mountain range, which extends over 18km east–west, was painted dozens of times by Paul Cézanne (1839–1906), who could see it from his home in Aix-en-Provence. The *castellum* of Aquae Sextiae had been founded in 122 BC by Caius Sextus Calvinus (*cos.* 124 BC) at the start of the campaigns that led to the annexation of Gallia Transalpina as a Roman *provincia* the following year (Liv. *Per.* 61.1, Strab. 4.1.5, Plin. 31.2.4) – i.e. a governmental area allotted to a Roman magistrate. Aquae Sextiae would become a Latin colony under Augustus. (Nicolas Brignol/Wikimedia Commons/ CC-BY-SA-3.0)

THE TEUTONES TAUNT THE ROMANS: MARIUS' CAMP AT AQUAE SEXTIAE, 102 BC (PP. 62–63)

For the Roman soldier, construction went hand-in-hand with campaigning. Any soldier hates cold and rain, yet the real bane of a legionary's life was digging. For the last two years Marius' men had spent more time wielding an axe or a pick than they did shouldering a *pilum* or drawing a *gladius*. While a daily drudgery, the overnight marching camp did give the men peace of mind knowing that they had a safe place to retreat to if needed. Likewise, it provided a relatively safe place to sleep – passing the night behind guarded ramparts kept the army from any more mental or physical fatigue than necessary.

Generally speaking, the site for the camp needed to be open, preferably on rising ground and with no cover that could be exploited by the enemy. The camp itself would cover an area of around four *plethra* (700m²) for a consular army of four legions. With Marius' army reforms, as well as the required digging tools, each legionary now carried one or two sharpened stakes, usually cut from sturdy branches. These were planted close together in the top of a low earth and turf rampart (*agger*) to form a sufficient palisade (*vallum*). To the front was a broad V-shaped ditch. Although these defences offered protection against surprise attack, the ditch and palisaded rampart were sufficient only to delay attackers and not to stop them. The Romans rarely, if ever, planned to fight

from within their camp, and instead sought to advance and meet the enemy in the field.

Marius' camp between the Rhodanus and Isara rivers, on the other hand, was of a more permanent nature, as witnessed by a palisaded rampart here (**1**). The turf-revetted rampart, with its more sturdy palisade of planks or hurdles, was studded with timber observation towers and pierced by four gateways, and fronted a double-ditch system. Sharpened forked branches (*cervi*) were firmly embedded in the top of the earthwork so they projected horizontally to prevent any attempt to scale it. Behind these substantial defences the Romans idle, or so it seems to the Teutones beyond (**2**). Fierce, proud, and fearless, a group of Teutones try to tempt the Romans out by whistles, boos, catcalls, and jeers. Lucius Cornelius Sulla (**3**), one of Marius' *legati*, provides reassurances to his legionaries, accompanied by two centurions, one of whom holds a vine staff (**4**).

In the background, heading south-eastwards and away from the Roman camp, four-wheeled wagons and two-wheeled carts drawn by draft animals carry the kinfolk and chattels of the fighting men (**5**). In their wake trudge the communal livestock tended by the adolescent Teutones. It is an engorged, sluggish caravan strung out for miles as it traverses the waning afternoon – people, oxen, cattle, mules, wagons, and carts.

Judging it necessary before engaging in battle to do something which would dispel the panic into which fear of the enemy had thrown his army, like a prudent general, he more than once stationed his army in a position near to which the army of the Cimbri [*sic*] must pass, with the intention that from behind the fortifications of their camp, his troops should look at and accustom their eyes to the enemy's appearance, so that they saw what a disorderly crowd they were, encumbered with baggage, their arms useless and some without arms, they might be reassured and become eager for the fight.

Machiavelli *Discorsi* 3.37

As for the Ambrones accompanying the Teutones, they were most likely a Germanic tribe (cf. Oros. 5.16.1, who says they were from Gaul) from the same northern neighbourhood as the Cimbri and Teutones.

First blood

Having dogged the Teutones and Ambrones since they crossed the Rhodanus, Marius moved into the vicinity of the *castellum* of Aquae Sextiae. Once belonging to the Salluvii, a Ligurian people, Aquae Sextiae happened to be the first Roman foundation in Gallia Transalpina.

No Roman army slept unprotected, and at the end of the day's march, Marius followed the habitual Roman custom and began to establish a fortified camp, which in this case was to be on high ground overlooking a river. Following the usual order of things, four military tribunes would have overseen the construction of the camp's four walls, thrown up from the spoil dug from the V-shaped ditches surrounding the camp. Legionaries would have been doing the manual work under the direction of their centurions, while the allied cavalry and lightly armed troops stood ready to drive off any attack.

As the soldiers laboured, servants and slaves went down the slope to the river to fetch water. They went armed, of course, with swords, axes, and spears, since the Germanic encampment lay just across the river and some of

Following Marius' reforms the legionaries now had to shoulder much of their gear: bedroll and cloak, three or more days' rations of grain, a bronze cooking pot (*trulleus*) and mess tin (*patera*), a leather flask, a sickle (*falx*) for cutting grain and forage, a wicker basket (*sporta*) for earth moving, either a pickaxe (*dolabra*) or an iron-shod wooden spade (*pala*), a length of rope, a tough leather satchel (*loculus*) for personal belongings, and a sharpened stake (*pilum muralis*) for fortifying the overnight marching camp. This gear, collectively known as the *sarcina*, was slung from a T-shaped carrying pole (*furca*), and Plutarch writes the soldiers were nicknamed *muli Mariani*, a wry description that would remain in popular currency. Each eight-man *contubernium* on the march was also allowed one four-legged mule to carry the heavier items, such as its leather tent and millstones. (MatthiasKabel/Wikimedia Commons/CC-BY-SA-2.5)

Full-scale reconstructions of an *aquila* and a *signum* (Alise-Sainte-Reine, MuséoParc Alésia). First introduced by Marius, the most important standard of the legion was the *aquila*, a silver statuette of an eagle perched on a long shaft. In addition to the *aquila*, legions carried secondary standards, whereby each individual century was identified by its own *signum*. While there are seemingly endless small variations to these depicted in the sculptural and numismatic evidence, *signa* were basically an assemblage of *phalerae* (discs) mounted on a pole surmounted by a spearhead, as shown here, or *manus* (effigy hand). The latter was probably originally associated with the maniple, viz. *manipulus* or 'handful'. (© Esther Carré)

the enemy were down at the water themselves. It may not have been unusual for opponents to meet each other under such circumstances, each side tacitly putting up with the other so long as they could keep apart. On the other hand, sometimes a scuffle would erupt, as happened this day. The Ambrones left their encampment to help their fellows at the water's edge, and some contingents of *socii*, local Ligurians in the main, and Romans went down the hill to meet them as they splashed across the river. Plutarch tells us that the Ambrones, 'gorged with food ... and intoxicated with strong drink' (*Mar.* 19.3), suffered a significant defeat, but he may have exaggerated as the larger and decisive engagement was fought two days later. He does, however, say 'that the battle by the river took place rather by accident than by design of the general' (ibid. 19.7).

Accident or not, this fracas meant the Romans were unable to complete their fortifications before nightfall. They still held the heights where the half-finished camp lay, and the enemy had retired, but the security the soldiers were accustomed to – and upon which the commander relied to keep his men rested and confident – was not there. This would be a night of little ease. But fortunately for Marius and his men there was no attack during the night. The enemy evidently had had enough fighting during the brisk engagement down at the river, and they spent the next day getting ready for the coming battle. Marius did likewise, putting a number of *cohortes*, perhaps five or six with one taken from each legion – they are said to have numbered 3,000 men in all – under one of his *legati*, a certain Marcus Claudius Marcellus,[8] and ordered him to slip silently into a wooded area nearby and hold his men there throughout the night in preparation for battle the following day (Plut. *Mar.* 20.4). Frontinus adds some further detail at this point, saying:

> [To] complete the illusion of a large force, [Marius] ordered armed grooms and camp followers to go along with them, and also a large part of the pack animals, wearing saddlecloths, in order by this means to present the appearance of cavalry.
>
> Frontin. 2.4.6

Marcellus and his men were destined to perform a vital role in the closing stages of the coming event. With Plutarch saying that the rest of the Roman soldiers got 'a good night's sleep' (*Mar.* 20.4), we can safely assume that they had managed to complete their camp.

The balance of the army Marius led out the next morning, and by deploying in front of the camp he kept securely to the height above the river. At the same time, he dispatched his cavalry down into the plain so as to skirmish with the enemy and provoke them into action. We do not know the disposition of the legionaries, though it is assumed that they were formed up in the conventional *triplex acies*.

---

8   He was perhaps the father of another Marcus Claudius Marcellus, *curule aedile* of 91 BC mentioned by Cicero (*Orat.* 1.57). If so, then he was the grandfather of two later consuls, yet another Marcus Claudius Marcellus (*cos.* 51 BC) and his brother Caius Claudius Marcellus (*cos.* 49 BC), both zealous opponents of Iulius Caesar.

A commander's place during battle must be where the most critical decisions are being taken. On this day, Marius judged rightly that the most difficult task lay with the legionaries, many of whom, such as the *capite censi*, were facing combat for the first time. Consequently, to put heart into his soldiers, Marius opted to place himself in the front rank of the fighting line, relying on his own fitness and skill at arms to show to his men that their general would share every danger with them from the onset of the action (Plut. *Mar.* 20.6).

It is worth noting at this point that any Roman commander worth his salt, although he normally stationed himself close behind the fighting line, did not habitually emulate the bellicose behaviour of a Homeric hero by rashly engaging in hand-to-hand combat. His principal responsibility was to encourage his *centuriones* and *milites*, and tightly control the fighting line to his front. Of course, the knowledge that Marius was prepared to share many of the grave realities of combat helped to inspire his men. Bravery, or the perception that one was brave, was a crucial component in the skill set of a successful Roman commander. More to the point, Marius understood that his men were about to face the *furor Teutonicus*.

Punch, jab

Just prior to the thick of the action, as Plutarch records, Marius ordered his legionaries to stand firm against the oncoming Teutones and 'hurl their javelins … and then to draw their swords and force them backwards with their shields' (*Mar.* 20.5). The instruction to discharge 'javelins' (*akóntion* in Plutarch's Greek) and then join battle with sword and shield is such as we might expect to be given to an army that had adopted the *pilum* and *gladius Hispaniensis*. Likewise, if this is so, the offensive use of the *scutum* tells us that the tactical doctrine commonly associated with the Roman army of the Principate was now firmly in place. The only difference, of course, was that the legionaries were to stand fast and receive the enemy charge instead of them advancing. Obviously Marius thought it prudent to await the enemy's inevitable onslaught from his superior position and then advance down the slope once the enemy had been disordered and disconcerted.

Much like the riot shield of modern police, the *scutum* was used both defensively and offensively to deflect blows and hammer into the opponent's shield or body to create openings for the *gladius*. As he stood with his left foot forward, a legionary could get much of his body weight behind this punch. Added to this was the considerable weight of the *scutum* itself. Weights of reconstructions range from 5.5kg to 10kg (the Republican model being heavier than that of the Principate), and a hefty punch delivered with the weight of the body behind the left hand stood a good chance of overbalancing an opponent.

Needless to say, men do not automatically lie down and expire when another man sticks a sword into them. The human hide is surprisingly sturdy. Considerable force is required to drive a blade into a person, and it is almost as difficult to pull it out. While a slashing sword might kill a man outright if very

Full-scale reconstruction of the Italic oval, semi-cylindrical body shield, conventionally known as the *scutum*, used by legionaries of the late Republic (Aquileia, Taberna Marciani). The *scutum* was made of three alternating layers of birch plywood, covered in leather and finished with a central iron boss and an edging of iron. By Caesar's day, as attested by sculptural evidence, the unadorned leather outer face was clearly decorated with designs and perhaps colours, which may possibly have indicated the bearer's unit. The necessity of unit identification by shield motif seems a logical development during the recurrent civil wars of the late Republic. (© Esther Carré)

Note: gridlines are shown at intervals of 250m (273 yards)

TEUTONES/AMBRONES
A. Warriors
B. Laagered encampment

xxxx
TEUTOBOD

ARC RIVER

▼ **EVENTS**

1. Marius deploys his five or six legions in front of the Roman camp, ordering his legionaries to hold fast and stand their ground.

2. At the same time, the Roman cavalry are sent down into the plain to provoke the Teutones and Ambrones into action.

3. The Teutones and Ambrones form large, solid wedges and begin to surge up the limestone heights towards the Roman position.

4. Having discharged their *pila*, the legionaries, with *scuta* and *gladii*, force the warriors back down the slope.

5. Sensing the time is right, Marcellus leads his five or six cohorts out of their concealment and into the rear of the fully engaged Northerners.

6. The victorious Romans pursue the broken Northerners all the way to the laagered encampment.

TRIAL BY COMBAT – AQUAE SEXTIAE 102 BC

Having shadowed the Northerners since the first encounter with them at the confluence of the Isara with the Rhodanus, Marius has decided to force the issue not far from the Roman *castellum* of Aquae Sextiae. The coming battle will be the first genuine test for the *muli Mariani*.

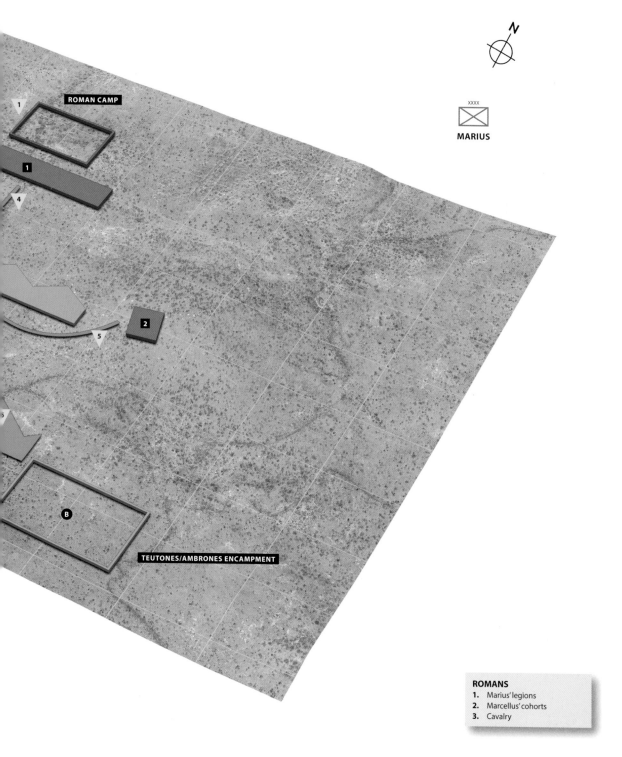

ROMANS
1. Marius' legions
2. Marcellus' cohorts
3. Cavalry

skilfully wielded – head, left shoulder, and left upper arm being the most vulnerable – it was more likely to cause a wound that would gradually prove fatal, either through the loss of blood or a subsequent bacterial infection. But in the savage intimacy of close combat, one well directed upward thrust from a *gladius* could extinguish life within a heartbeat.

Such an extraordinary long sword, and blunt-ended to boot, required a warrior to have a fair amount of elbow room on the field of battle in order to operate proficiently. Nonetheless, those who could expertly swing one of these made fearsome opponents for other mortals, and even the most grizzled, battle-hardened legionary veteran would likely become a bit windy if a sword-swinging warrior got close enough to slash him, and rightly so. Still, however devastating the first sword stroke, time and strength were required to disengage and raise the slashing sword for a second stroke. The push of the *gladius* by comparison expended minimal time, effort, and motion, thus allowing it to be withdrawn and easily recovered in a moment. In a congested struggle this consideration would prove critical. Additionally, employing the thrust meant the legionary kept most of his torso well covered, and thus protected, by his *scutum*. The slashing sword was dreadful, but the *gladius* proved grimly lethal: a man dies fast. To echo the spot-on evaluation of Vegetius (1.12): the grindstone-sharpened edge of a slashing sword cut; the long, lethal point of the *gladius* killed. All this is more easily described than accomplished. Being a good swordsman required doggedness and diligence.

Following Marius' reforms, the Romans would attach a great deal of importance to weapon training, and it is this that largely explains the success of their army. 'And what can I say about the training of legions?' is the rhetorical question aired by Cicero. 'Put an equally brave, but untrained soldier in the front line, and he will look like a woman' (*Tusc.* 2.16.37). The basic goal of this training was to give the Romans superiority (viz. qualitative advantage) over the barbarians (viz. quantitative advantage) in battle, hence the legionary was taught to attack with the *gladius* by thrusting and not by slashing. The better beats the many.

Roman swordsmanship was to become a fully developed art with a comprehensive system of practices and techniques, and it was in our period that the basic system of training in the use of the *gladius* was developed and refined. Basic swordsmanship techniques can be divided into three major groups: cuts, thrusts, and parries. The training programme for legionaries was both rigorous and continuous. It was based upon repeated drills, which not only developed the outer factors of the art (viz. technique and accuracy), but the inner ones (viz. control and balance), too.

A final point: a legionary carried his *gladius* on the right-hand side and was suspended by a leather belt (*cingulum*) worn around the waist. As opposed to a scabbard-slide, the four-ring

The well-preserved blade of a *gladius* (Saint-Germain-en-Laye, Musée d'archéologie nationale, inv. 49824) found at Trévoux (*département* of Ain). The blade shows a length of 610mm including the handgrip, the blade itself measuring 479mm. This sword belongs to the first of two models of *gladius*, the long-pointed 'Mainz' type. With its superb two-edged blade and lethal triangular point, legionaries were trained to thrust, not slash, with this particularly murderous weapon: a short stab in the soft belly of an opponent was enough to incapacitate him. (© Esther Carré)

suspension system on the scabbard enabled the legionary to draw his weapon quickly with the right hand, an asset in fighting at close quarters in the chaotic but decisive end phase of battle. Inverting the right hand to grasp the hilt and then pushing the pommel forward drew the *gladius* with certain ease.

The battle

As you would expect, the initiative of the attack gives to the assailant a certain moral influence. But with trusted soldiers, duly trained, a general can try a stratagem, and Marius' men had spent the good part of the past couple of years training and conditioning. Having been ordered by Marius to stand fast in the face of the enemy attack, the *muli Mariani* were about to prove their dependability by calmly waiting on the spot, without stirring, for a vigorous enemy hell-bent on their destruction. Marius, who was as close to being a career soldier as anyone in the Late Republic, had not been slow to recognize the defensive potential of the limestone ridge of high ground upon which his army had constructed its marching camp. The ridge was made all the more prominent by the otherwise open setting it dominated.

Not short on bravery and determination, the Teutones and Ambrones attacked uphill in a limestone landscape made more challenging by its broken nature. In all probability out of breath and in some disarray, they were met with a lethal hail of *pila*. Buckling under the bombardment, the Northerners recoiled and were driven slowly back down the slope by the disciplined advance of the legionaries. To make matters worse, while fully engaged on the lower slope of the limestone ridge, the Northerners were struck from behind by Marcellus' cohorts. These legionaries had emerged from their arboreal hiding place where they had been biding their time while their comrades performed their cruel duty. Frontinus includes 'the sutlers, servants, and camp followers of every sort', and so Marcellus 'threw the enemy into panic by giving the appearance of having a large army' (2.4.8). At that pivotal moment, the enemy, pinioned between two forces and suffering terribly, dissolved and was wholly defeated.

Saint-Pons, a 14th-century bridge that traverses the Arc River west of Aix-en-Provence. It was on high ground above this river that Marius pitched his camp prior to the battle of Aquae Sextiae. According to Frontinus, Marius deliberately chose the spot because 'the barbarians controlled the water supply', so encouraging his hot and thirsty soldiers to drive 'the barbarians from the place' (2.7.12). For any army in any age, potable water is an indispensable resource. A Roman soldier on campaign needed a daily water ration per man of at least 2.25 litres to prevent dehydration (by comparison, the US forces involved in the 1990–91 Gulf War required at least 10 litres per day), while a horse required roughly 19 to 57 litres of water per day, depending on the temperature. (Mathieu Brossais/Wikimedia Commons/ CC-BY-SA-4.0)

General view of the village of Pourrières, *département* of Var, from the Chemin Saint-Pierre. The village lies in the rolling plain beneath Mount Sainte-Victoire (visible in the left distance) and is 27km from Aix-en-Provence. Its name, according to tradition, derives from the Latin *Campi Putridi* (Fr. *pourrir*, 'to rot'), so-named after the corpses of the Teutones and the Ambrones fertilizing the local soil as a result of the battle of Aquae Sextiae. Just south of the village runs the Arc River, which may be the watercourse where the watering parties of the opposing armies came to blows prior to the main engagement. (Christian Amet/Wikimedia Commons/CC-BY-SA-2.5)

In their pursuit of the broken Northerners, the Romans overran and pillaged their laagered encampment across the river, and in doing so 'seized their tents, wagons, and their property' (Plut. *Mar.* 21.2). The usual incredible figures are given for the killed and captured (Liv. *Per.* 68.3, Vell. 2.12.4), and putting hard numbers on the butcher's bill is tricky when the information comes from Graeco-Roman sources. However, whatever the exact figures, the Teutones and the Ambrones had been reduced to a gory shambles and, as a result, were finally finished as a threat to Rome (Flor. 1.38.11).

Aftermath

Of course, we should never forget there were the dead, those unburied corpses which marked the killing zone and whose pungent fug stuck to garments and hair. Tens of thousands of men, women, children, and horses died, and a gruesome question remains: what happened to the dead bodies at Aquae Sextiae? On this particular point, Plutarch has the following story to tell:

> [It] is said that the people of Massilia [modern Marseille] fenced their vineyards round with the bones and that the soil where the dead bodies, soaked in the rain which fell throughout the winter, had rotted away was fertilized to a considerable depth by the putrefied matter and became so rich that it yielded in future years quite extraordinary harvests, thus justifying the saying by Archilochos [a mid-7th-century BC Parian soldier poet] that 'in such ways the fields are fattened'.[9]
>
> Plut. *Mar.* 21.3

---

9 Archilochos fr. 148 Edmonds: πρὸς τοῦ τοιούτου δ' ἤροσις πιαίνεται / With such corpses the fields are fattened.

The surviving warriors, along with their dependents, were sold into slavery. Normally the proceeds of the sale of slaves belonged solely to the general, but on this occasion Marius opted to donate the money to his legates, tribunes, centurions, and men (Plut. *Mar*. 21.2–3) – a popular gesture, without doubt.

VERCELLAE, 101 BC

Cimbri deleti / The Cimbri were destroyed

Iulius Obsequens 44a

Boïorix, the war leader of the Cimbri, had chosen to lead his people via an indirect route into the Italian peninsula by marching around the northern foothills of the Alps. This was achieved probably by heading up the Rhodanus to Lacus Lemanus (Lake Geneva) on the north side of the Alps. The Cimbri, in the event, 'had already descended during the winter (which increases the height of the Alps) from the Tridentine ranges like an avalanche into Italy' (Flor. 1.38.11). Plutarch's prose is rather more theatrical, assuring us that the warriors 'went naked' and 'came tobogganing down on their broad shields, sliding over the slippery slopes and the deep crevasses' (*Mar*. 23.3). Naked or not, a winter passage may seem odd to us, but as Napoleon, who had swept over the Alps into northern Italy on 20 May 1800 astride a sturdy mule and wearing a simple grey waistcoat, once explained:

> The winter is not the most unfavourable season for the passage of lofty mountains. The snow is then firm, the weather settled, and there is nothing to fear from avalanches, the real and only danger to be apprehended in the Alps.

Besides, the lowest of the great Alpine passes is the Brenner Pass (elev. 1,375m), and the flat broad saddle of the Brenner was the likely route the Cimbri negotiated on their southwards winter trek. It is first mentioned in our literary sources when Augustus ordered Nero Claudius Drusus, his stepson, to construct a useable road across the Eastern Alpine range, a strategic shortcut from Gallia Cisalpina to the upper reaches of the Rhenus, eliminating the detour via the Rhodanus. This was in 15 BC, and what would become the Via Claudia Augusta, connecting Verona with Augusta Vindelicorum (Augsburg) in Rhaetia, would be completed in AD 46 during the reign of Claudius, the son of Drusus.

Initial contact

Having successfully negotiated the passage of the Alps, the Cimbri then proceeded to give Quintus Lutatius Catulus a rough handling. He had the mission to guard the Alpine passes into Gallia Cisalpina. This he failed to achieve. It appears the Cimbri just rolled over the defences that Catulus had erected either side of the Athesis (Adige) River, which prompted the majority of his soldiers to depart their main camp post haste. In his *commentarii*, now lost but widely used by Plutarch, the consul wrote the episode up as a tactical retreat, with himself leading his men to safety (Plut. *Mar*. 23.4–5, cf. *Sull*. 4.2–3): we wonder how much Catulus owed his successful flight to the more experienced Sulla, his senior *legatus*. Calculated or not, the outcome allowed

The Adige valley, Trentino-Alto Adige, Italy, viewed from La Paganella (elev. 2,125m), a mountain of the Rhaetian Alps, with the pinnacles of the Dolomites to the east in the background. In the late winter/early spring of 101 BC, the Cimbri, despite their alleged nakedness, rapidly descended into Gallia Cisalpina along the Alpine valley of the upper Adige (Athesis) River. It was here they met, and sorely compromised, the consular army of Quintus Lutatius Catulus. (Gabri80/Wikimedia Commons/CC-BY-SA-3.0)

the Cimbri to break into the Italian peninsula. Here they spent the winter of 102/101 BC camped in Venetia, where they enjoyed, amongst other things, 'the delights of wine' (Flor. 1.38.14).

At the end of 102 BC, Marius was summoned to Rome by the Senate to discuss the worsening situation. According to Cassius Dio:

> After his victory at Aquae Sextiae, Marius so won over the nobles who had hated him that he was praised to the sky by the highborn and commoners alike. He was elected consul for the coming year [his fifth] to finish off the job with the willing and consenting support of the nobles.
>
> Dio 27 F94.1

Forgoing his triumph for Aquae Sextiae (Liv. *Per.* 68.5) – he had already been voted a second one – Marius readily agreed to join his army with that of Catulus in the north. The Cimbri, not knowing of Aquae Sextiae, were awaiting the arrival of the Teutones before engaging the combined armies of Rome, and so were initially unwilling to join battle. Marius was only too happy to show them the enchained Teutobod, the war leader of the Teutones (Plut. *Mar.* 24.3–4). The die being cast, the Cimbri prepared for a set battle.

The location

As every soldier will testify, every battlefield is *sui generis* in its details. This leads to the vexed question: where were the Cimbri defeated? The

fascination of the question can be imagined, especially for those of us who enjoy yomping across ancient battlefields, ancient literature in hand. Plutarch speaks of the plain of Vercellae (τό πεδίον τό περὶ Βερκέλλας, *Mar.* 25.5), while the Latin authors refer to the *Campi Raudii* or the *Campus Raudius* (Vell. 2.12.5, Flor. 1.38.14, *Vir. ill.* 67.2). Still, the actual identity of this location is a matter of academic debate. The majority of scholars favour Plutarch and accordingly argue for a site close to the city now called Vercelli in Piedmont.

Others, however, plausibly argue that the battle was fought near the Po delta between the modern towns of Rovigo and Ferrara. Take for example Ernst Badian (1962: p. 217):

> The campaign of Vercellae has been notably clarified by Zennari's scholarly investigations of the meaning of the word (a Celtic word, denoting a spot where metal could be mined, and therefore a common place name – 'Campi Raudii' apparently has a similar meaning) and localization of the Vercellae of the battle on the lower Po near Rovigo: the statue of Marius at Ravenna (Plut. *Mar.* 2.1) is probably connected with this. This study makes all earlier discussions of the battle – or later ones written in ignorance of it – obsolete.

It was Jacopo Zennari (1956), using inscriptions, literary texts, and mediaeval documents to bolster his thesis, who pointed out that there were several places in the Po basin known as *vercellae*. The word is of Celtic origin and indicated areas of mineral workings between streams where there were deposits of gold or other minerals – and thus Strabo's remark 'there was a gold mine at Vercellae' (5.1.12). Zennari considered the word *raudus* as Celtic, too, possibly referring to the reddish colour caused by iron deposits. The Cimbri,

Panoramic view of the city of Vercelli, Piedmont, against a backdrop of the Western Alps. Traditionally, historians locate the battle of Vercellae near Vercelli, possibly at Borgo Vercelli 5km to the north-east and close to the right bank of the Sesia (Sessites) River, a tributary of the Po (Padus). Vercellae was the chief *oppidum* of the Libici, a Ligurian people in Gallia Cisalpina. In the time of Strabo (5.1.12) it was an unfortified village, but by Tacitus' day (*Hist.* 1.70) was a strong Roman *municipium* (founded in 49 BC). Here the road from Ticinum to Augusta Praetoria was crossed by a road running west from Mediolanum (Milan). (Blusea/Wikimedia Commons/CC-BY-SA-3.0)

The Adige as it enters the Polesine near Badia Polesine, north-east Italy. The Polesine is a flat, fertile strip of land between the lower courses of the Adige (Athesis) and Po (Padus) rivers and the Adriatic Sea (Mare Adriaticum). A small number of historians think that the battle of Vercellae could have been fought in this area, possibly near the modern town of Rovigo, Veneto. Instead of irrationally turning and rolling inexorably west, if we follow this line of reasoning, the Cimbri continued southwards down the Athesis towards the Padus. (Franco2005rsm/ Wikimedia Commons/ Public domain)

in that case, having negotiated the Rhaetian Alps (Alpes Rhaeticae), did not turn west but marched *down* the Adige (Athesis) and towards the Po (Padus). This is a highly plausible line of reasoning, and one that I favour.

The battle

The battle took place 'three days before the new moon [Kalends] of the month now called August, but then Sextilis' (Plut. *Mar.* 26.4). Unsurprisingly for the time of year, it being after the summer solstice, dawn broke with misty conditions (Flor. 1.38.15), forecasting that the day was going to be an extremely hot one. Opting to take the offensive, Marius, who had divided the 32,000 men (six legions, perhaps) of his consular army between the two wings, had his soldiers advance through the dust and haze. He, presumably, was commanding the right wing, while Catulus, with Sulla acting as his senior *legatus*, held the centre together with his consular army, which was one-third smaller than that of Marius', having only 20,300 men (four legions, perhaps). These figures, which are unusually precise, Plutarch (*Mar.* 25.3) says he obtained from Sulla's *commentarii*. As for the commander of the left wing, Plutarch does not say, but a good guess would be Marcus Claudius Marcellus, who had clearly earned his salt as Marius' *legatus* the previous year at Aquae Sextiae.

The Cimbri were suffering not only from the skin-burning, blistering heat, but also from the glare of the sun as it rose towards its noontime position. As Frontinus reports, Marius had wisely arranged 'his own line of battle so that the barbarians were caught with the sun and wind and dust in their faces'

(2.2.8), that is to say, 'he had drawn up his line facing the west' (Flor. 1.38.15). According to Plutarch, and presumably despite the obvious discomfort from the unfavourable conditions, the Cimbri nonetheless started to advance towards the Romans in a solid block '30 stadia in extent' (*Mar.* 25.6), which is an incredible 6km. The warriors were supported by no fewer than 15,000 horsemen, all magnificently clad in helmets and body armour (taken from Roman corpses?), and though not stated, they were probably in front as they were the first into action. They attacked on the Roman right, where Marius' cavalry were stationed. Their intention was to trap it between themselves and their own foot warriors. A swift counter-attack by the Roman horsemen, however, pushed the enemy well away from the Roman battle line.

To their utter consternation, the Romans, having hurled their *pila*, suddenly charged upon them from the east, and 'the sky seemed to be on fire with the glint reflected from the bronze of the Roman helmets' (Flor. 1.38.15, cf. Oros. 5.16.15). Sensing their sudden uneasiness, it appears the Romans decided to take the initiative. In the ferocious struggle that followed, the best of the Cimbri were scythed down:

> [For] in order to preserve an unbroken line those who were fighting in the front ranks were fastened together by long chains which were passed through their belts.

Plut. *Mar.* 27.1

Battaglia di Vercelli (New York, Metropolitan Museum of Art, inv. 65.183.3), oil on canvas (1729) by Giovanni Battista Tiepolo. Another of his ten monumental canvases painted to decorate the *salone* of the Ca' Dolfin, Venice, this one celebrates Marius' victory over the Cimbri at Vercellae. While his art was firmly based on the exaltation of the artist's imagination over historical accuracy – he was the victim of the decorative tastes of his age – the imperfect magnificence of Marius struck a cord with Tiepolo. (Metropolitan Museum of Art/Wikimedia Commons/CC0 1.0)

Any of the unchained Cimbri who managed to escape this mayhem and reach the apparent sanctuary of their laagered camp were to be disappointed. For they were slain by their womenfolk before they, as various sources tell us (Plut. *Mar.* 27.2, Vell. 2.12.4–5, Flor. 1.38.16–18, Oros. 5.16.17–18), committed mass infanticide and suicide.

It is reported by Plutarch (*Mar.* 27.3, cf. Liv. *Per.* 68.5, Oros. 5.16.17–19, Flor. 1.38.15) that no fewer than 120,000 of their warriors were cut to pieces and 60,000 were captured. On the face of it these seem rather absurd figures, but as T.F. Carney argues, 'as the deaths of women and children are recounted they must be included in the total of killed and captured by Plutarch' (1958: p. 231, n. 13).

Among the dead was the Cimbri war leader Boïorix. Caesar notes that in times of war, Germanic tribes would select what he calls a *magistratus* 'to preside over that war with such authority, that they have power of life and death' (*B Gal.* 6.23.4). As Tacitus says, the Germani 'take their kings [*reges*] on the grounds of birth, their war leaders [*duces*] on the basis of courage' (*Germ.* 7.1). This did not

THE BATTLE OF VERCELLAE 101 BC (PP. 78–79)

The Cimbri commence their ferocious onslaught at Vercellae with their war cries and suggestive taunts, a stratagem obviously employed to unnerve the opposition. The *barritus* is an undulating war cry that begins from silence and starts with a low murmuring that gradually crescendos to a loud roaring, the warriors 'putting their shields to their mouth, so that, by reverberation, it may swell into a fuller and deeper sound' (Tac. *Germ.* 3.2, cf. Veg. 3.18.9–10).

Plutarch says the Cimbri 'came sweeping on like a great ocean on the move', and adds that their front-rank warriors (**1**), who were obviously the best of the bunch, 'were fastened together by long chains (**2**) which were passed through their belts' (*Mar.* 26.2, 27.1). In the meantime, the Romans (**3**) stick to their strict observance of silence, and as long as Marius (**4**) leads them, they show little fear. Their general is an old campaigner who eats what they eat, shares their hardships, and knows war as they know it. As he had done the previous year at Aquae Sextiae, Marius sets a brave example to his men by positioning himself in the fighting line. He is bareheaded and carries a *scutum* (**5**). Two chosen centurions (**6**) shield him with their *scuta*. On this occasion, the tight discipline and tactical cohesion of the retrained and reorganized Roman legionaries will prove decisive.

A number of the Germanic warriors, particularly in the front ranks, are equipped with Roman war gear (**7**). Following their previous victories over Roman armies, particularly those two at Arausio, such items as *gladii*, *loricae hamata*, and Montefortino helmets were stripped from dead or captured legionaries. Other warriors have picked up La Tène D long slashing swords during their extensive peregrinations around Gaul. On the other hand, virtually the only defensive arm for the vast majority of the warriors is a simple shield (**8**), flat, long, and oval or rectangular. The shield boss – often, though not invariably, of iron – is frequently prominent enough to be used as an offensive weapon, to be thrust at the face of an unlucky opponent. Both wickerwork and wooden shields were reported, some of the better constructed ones being covered with leather and bound with bronze strips at their edges.

Even when not migrating, the Germani went to war in the company of their friends and family; even women and children accompanied them, to minister to their needs, to bind their wounds, to rouse their valour, and to scold their weakness. They would remain at the laagered encampment of the Cimbri, offering their vocal support to their fighting menfolk as they were about to clash with the enemy.

mean that a king could not be a war leader, only that the position of a king had a quite different societal basis from that of a war leader. The latter owed his position to his ability as a leader of warriors and he could only maintain it by a record of battlefield success. Predictably, Germanic society was a warrior society, a society geared to waging war, within tribes, between different peoples, and against external enemies. Naturally, in battle, the war leader led from the front, fighting side by side with his immediate family members. For as Tacitus reports:

> On the field of battle it is a disgrace to a chief [*principe*] to be surpassed in courage by his retinue [*comites*], and to the retinue not to equal the courage of their chief. And to leave a battle alive after a chief has fallen means lifelong infamy and shame. To defend and protect him, and to let him get credit for their own acts of heroism, are the most solemn obligations of their allegiance. The chiefs fight for victory, the retinue for their chief.
>
> Tac. *Germ.* 14.1

By all accounts, Boïorix heroically fell in this battle, fighting furiously and slaying many of his opponents (Flor. 1.38.18, cf. Oros. 5.16.20). He, along with his retinue, must have fought with the undiluted courage of the doomed.

Lob, puncture

The *hastati* of the pre-Marian legion carried both a light and a heavy *pilum* as part of their offensive armament. Polybios distinguishes two types of *pilum* (ὑσσός/*hyssós* in his Greek), 'thick' and 'thin', saying each man had both types. He describes their construction as follows:

> The length of the wooden shaft of them all is approximately three cubits [*c.* 135cm]. An iron head is fixed to each shaft that is barbed and of the same length as the shaft. They secure the head so firmly, attaching it halfway up the shaft and fixing it with several rivets, that the iron breaks in battle sooner than this fastening becomes loose, although its thickness at the socket is a finger and a half's breadth; such pains do they take about securing it firmly.
>
> Polyb. 6.23.10–12, cf. Veg. 1.20, 2.15

By Polybios' reckoning, the *pilum* had a barbed iron head, presumably hardened, at the end of a long iron shank, some 60cm to 90cm in length. This was fastened to a one-piece wooden shaft, for which ash was the preferred wood, though hazel, willow, poplar, and alder were also used. One type has the shank socketed, while the other has a wide, flat, iron tang riveted to a thickened section of the wooden shaft. The last type is almost certainly Polybios' 'thick' *pilum*, referring to the broad joint of iron and wood. This broad section can be either square or round in section, and is strengthened by a small iron ferrule.

The head was designed to puncture shield and armour, the long iron shank passing through the hole made by the hardened head. Once the weapon had struck home, or even if it missed and hit the ground, the shank tended to buckle and bend under the weight of the shaft. With its aerodynamic qualities destroyed, it could not be effectively thrown back, while if it lodged in a shield, it became extremely difficult to remove. Put simply, the *pilum*

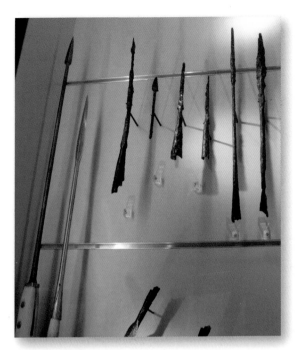

Pila heads (Alise-Sainte-Reine, MuséoParc Alésia) found at the site of Alésia, while on the left are full-scale replicas of a heavy *pilum* and a light *pilum*. Note some of the heads are pyramidal, while others are leaf-shaped. It was the heavy *pilum*, with its long, flat tang and two rivets, which was modified by Marius prior to the battle of Vercellae. This modification introduced an inbuilt weakness by replacing one of the two iron rivets, which fixed the iron shank to the wooden shaft, with a wooden dowel. The wooden dowel would snap upon impact, resulting in the iron shank bending because of the weight of the wooden shaft. (© Esther Carré)

would either penetrate flesh or become useless to the enemy. Modern experiments have shown that a *pilum*, thrown from a distance of 5m, could pierce 30mm of pine wood or 20mm of plywood (Bishop–Coulston 1993: p. 48). The maximum range of the *pilum* was some 30m, but its effective range was something akin to half that (Junkelmann 1991: p. 188). Unsurprisingly, throwing a *pilum* at close range improved both accuracy and armour penetration.

Plutarch (*Mar.* 25.1–2) attributes to Marius a modification of the junction between the iron shank and the wooded shaft. So as to make it more certain that the missile would bend on impact, Marius replaced one of the two iron rivets, which held the iron shank of the *pilum* to its wooden shaft, with a wooden dowel. With this modification the wooden dowel would snap upon impact, resulting in the *pilum* bending in such a way that, while the barbed head remained firmly embedded, the wooden shaft fell to the ground. Archaeological evidence from one of the five Roman camps east of the Iberian stronghold of Numantia indicates that it was the heavy *pilum* that was modified in this way. Similar examples were recovered from the site of the siege at Alésia (eastern France), showing both types of *pilum* were still in use in Caesar's day. Whereas a long, flat tang and two rivets were used for the heavier type, the lighter version was simply socketed onto its wooden shaft.

It should be understood that Plutarch specifically attributes this reform to preparations made for the coming confrontation with the Cimbri in 101 BC and not in conjunction with Marius' previous encounter against the Teutones and Ambrones at Aquae Sextiae the previous campaigning season. Based upon the time required to make the necessary alterations to the vast number of weapons carried by Marius' legionaries, it can only be concluded that the work done on modifying the heavy *pilum* was conducted some time after Aquae Sextiae but before Marius had reinforced Catulus in Gallia Cisalpina. In any period of history, it takes an enormous amount of equipment to sustain military operations. R.J. Forbes (1964: p. 96), citing Livy (1.43.3), Dionysios of Halikarnassos (7.59.1), and Cicero (*Rep.* 2.39), has calculated that a Roman army of eight legions (let us say around 40,000 men) required some 1,600 *fabri* (carpenters and smiths) to keep it prepared for battle. So, this particular Marian reform cannot have been a spur of the moment decision, but a planned alteration designed to negate an aspect of the Germanic mode of battle which Marius had seen in operation in 102 BC (Matthew 2010A: p. 53).

To be more specific, if a heavy *pilum* penetrated an opponent's shield, but did not kill him, the missile could only pass through the shield up to the point where the wooden block at the head of the shaft connected with the outer surface of the shield. The hole created by the tip would not have been large enough to allow the missile to penetrate any further.

Hence, the entire wooden shaft would remain on the outside of the shield while the head, on the inside of the shield, remained pointing directly at the bearer when the shield was held across his front. Plutarch (*Mar.* 25.2) clearly states that the unaltered *pilum* would project straight out of whatever it had transfixed. The weight and leverage of the projecting shaft would make the shield unwieldy and, depending upon where the shield had been pierced and the configuration of its grip, would pull the shield forward, exposing the bearer to attack.

Like the unaltered *pilum*, the tip of a Marian *pilum* which had penetrated an enemy shield would have remained pointing at the bearer, making a charge while bearing the shield a risky proposition. The weight of the swinging shaft would have similarly made the shield unwieldy. Where the Marian reform enhanced the functionality of the *pilum* was by ensuring that the shield could no longer be held across the front of the bearer. When the wooden dowel broke after it impacted on the shield of an opponent, the wooden shaft would swing on the remaining iron rivet downwards 'and trail along the ground, being held fast by the twist at the point of the weapon' (Plut. *Mar.* 25.2).

Mars, god of war, on the Altar of Domitius Ahenobarbus (Paris, musée du Louvre, inv. Ma 975) dressed in the uniform of a senior officer, most probably that of a *tribunus militum*, military tribune. He stands before an altar. Looking more Hellenistic than Roman, he wears a short muscled cuirass equipped with two rows of fringed *pteruges* (which was necessary for those who rode a horse), greaves, and a crested Etrusco-Corinthian helmet. A peculiar and perverted development of the closed Greek Corinthian helmet commonly worn by hoplites, this pattern was worn on top of the head in jockey fashion while preserving for decoration the now-redundant eyeholes and nasal guard of the original facial area. He also has a circular shield, a spear, and a sword, which he wears on the left side. The knotted sash around his waist probably denotes his rank. (© Esther Carré)

Note: gridlines are shown at intervals of 250m (273 yards)

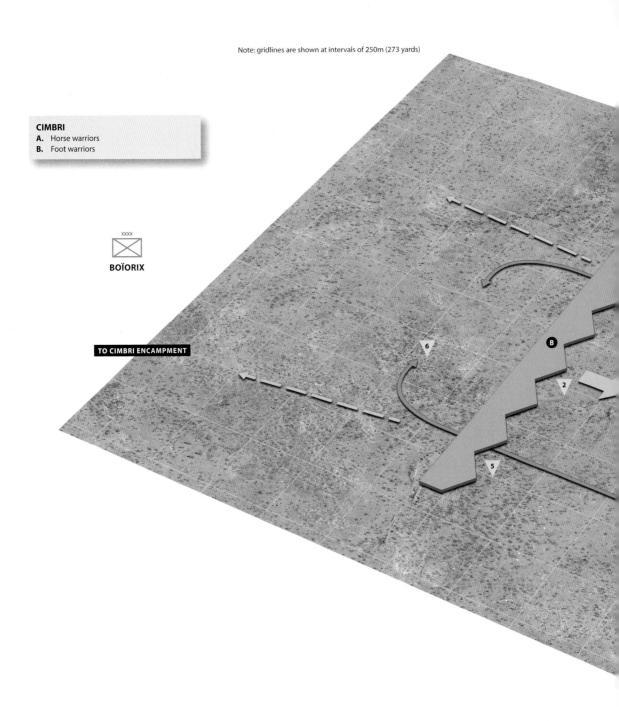

CIMBRI

A. Horse warriors
B. Foot warriors

BOÏORIX

TO CIMBRI ENCAMPMENT

▼ EVENTS

1. Marius deploys his six legions, three on each wing. He takes command of the right wing, while Marcus Claudius Marcellus commands the left. Catulus, with Sulla as his senior *legatus*, commands the centre with his four legions.

2. The Cimbri begin to surge forward in large, solid wedges, their best warriors forming the front ranks. As the Roman battleline faces west, the Cimbri have to face into the morning sun.

3. At the same time, the Cimbri horse warriors attempt to turn the Roman right, but are met and put to flight by the Roman cavalry.

4. The legionaries in the fighting line launch their *pila*, draw their *gladii*, and attack. The dust kicked up by tens of thousands of pounding feet flies into the faces of the Cimbri.

5. Marius' six legions, split between the two wings, rout their opponents and wheel in on the flanks of the Cimbri centre, which is still hotly engaged with Catulus' four legions.

6. Emerging from the dust and chaff, Marius' legions deal the final death blow to the Cimbri. Among the fallen is the war leader Boïorix, together with his retinue.

WAR COMES TO ITALIA – VERCELLAE 101 BC

Having joined forces with the recently embarrassed consular army of Catulus in Gallia Cisalpina, Marius prepares to overcome the last northern threat to Rome, the Cimbri. He intends to use the element of surprise, as well as the elements themselves, to his advantage.

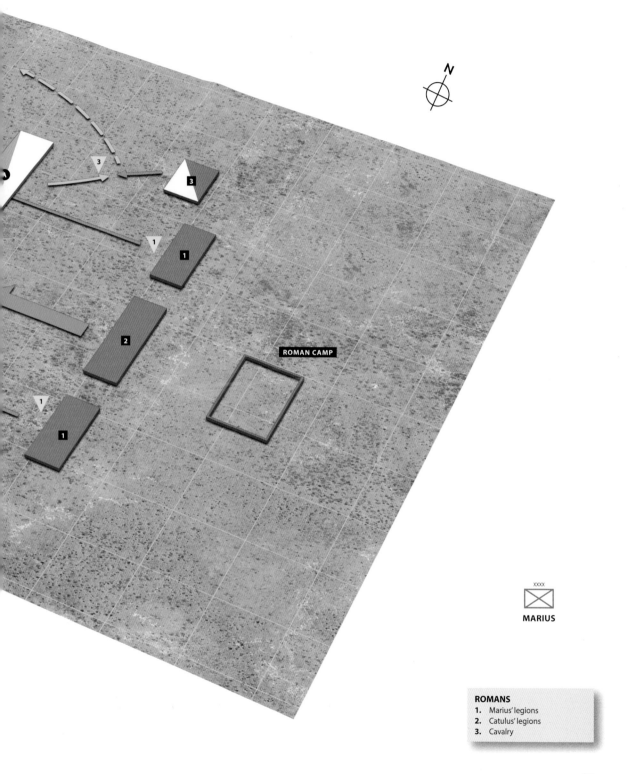

ROMAN CAMP

MARIUS

ROMANS
1. Marius' legions
2. Catulus' legions
3. Cavalry

This hanging wooden shaft would simply impede the motion of the legs, during any subsequent attempt to advance or charge.

As we would expect, Germanic warfare principally emphasized aggressive tactics on foot. Plutarch describes the Teutones at Aquae Sextiae as furiously rushing into contact in a configuration that was based on 'the locking of their shields' (*Mar.* 20.6). Marius may have expected the Cimbri to adopt a similar 'locked-shield' formation whenever the two sides eventually clashed, and made his alterations to the design of the heavy *pilum* after the battle of Aquae Sextiae to negate the strength of any Germanic shield-wall encountered in the future (Matthew 2010A: p. 58). Tacitus (*Germ.* 6.6, cf. *Hist.* 4.16.2, 5.16.1) mentions one particular formation as used by the Germani, the *cuneus* or wedge. He also adds:

> The strongest incentive to courage lies in this, that neither chance nor causal grouping makes the troop or the wedge [*turmam aut cuneum facit*], but family and kinship: close at hand, too, are their dearest, whence is heard the wailing voice of women and the child's cry: here are the witnesses who are in each man's eyes most precious.
>
> Tac. Germ. 7.3

In another place Tacitus describes the outnumbered Batavii as 'formed in wedges (*in cuneos congregantur*), presenting on every side a dense array, with fronts, flanks, and rear secure. Thus they were able to break the thin line of our soldiers' (*Hist.* 4.20.2). Writing some three centuries after Tacitus, Vegetius describes the *cuneus* as 'a mass of men on foot, in close formation, narrower in front, wider in the rear, that moves forwards and breaks the ranks of the enemy … soldiers call this formation *caput porcinum*' (3.19). Though it had limited offensive articulation, the wedge formation was a very effective formation when employed correctly.

The formation itself involved a mass of troops in a triangular wedge with the tip charging the enemy. The ensuing charge, if audaciously delivered, would penetrate into the ranks of the enemy and force them to fight individually, which was consistent with Germanic fighting philosophy. Still, breaking the enemy had to be done swiftly, in a single movement, otherwise the wedge could become surrounded and easily neutralized. The wedge had worked well against the maniple with its shallow ranks, but not so against the cohort.

As a point of interest, there was to be a final modification (often wrongly accredited to Caesar), whereby instead of having the whole iron shank tempered, the tempering was confined to the head. This ensured that the iron shank remained quite soft and liable to buckle and bend under the weight of the wooden shaft. As Caesar records on one occasion:

> Many of the Gauls were struck by the first discharge of weapons, and, as the iron had become bent, they were unable to draw them out, nor could they fight conveniently with their left arm thus additionally encumbered.
>
> Caes. B Gall. 1.25.3

As expected, having done their terrible work with *pila*, the front-line legionaries put their hands to *gladii*, the other murderous tool in their armoury, and got close enough to come to hand strokes with the surviving enemy and so finish the affair.

Aftermath

Though he made a point to celebrate a joint triumph with his fellow commander, the proconsul Catulus (Plut. *Mar.* 27.6, Cic. *Tusc.* 5.56), Marius claimed the whole credit for the victory at Vercellae. Equally, in popular thinking all the credit went to Marius (ibid. 27.5). The other two members of what was clearly an edgy trinity, Catulus and his *legatus* Sulla, on the other hand, gave very different accounts of the battle in their memoirs. Sulla, who had joined Marius and Catulus, for the northern war, naturally took the latter's side, and in his *commentarii* he dwells on the heroic actions of himself and his proconsular commander Catulus. This was not only out of a personal dislike of Marius but also because of a natural bias toward the senatorial aristocracy, whose dangerous and bloody champion he would later be.

Like any great man, Marius had more than his share of detractors. What is more, because Marius did not polish up his legacy by writing his *commentarii* – being neither a scholar nor philosopher – historians of the period have to rely upon those of his contemporaries: and they cast a hostile light on Marius. Three in particular, all consuls and unswerving *optimates* by conviction, were implacable foes whose careers diverged from that of Marius: Rutilius (Plut. *Mar.* 28.8), Catulus (App. *B civ.* 1.74), and Sulla (Plut. *Sull.* 6.2). The last, above all, was a *nobilis* who hailed from a patrician, albeit decayed, house and so thoroughly detested the *novus homo* Marius. It is highly probable, therefore, that the extant sources dealing with Marius and his extraordinary life reflect an anti-Marian tradition. An excellent example of Marius getting a thorough kicking in the memories of his enemy is to be found in the accounts dealing with this particular battle.

On reading Plutarch's account, our primary source for Vercellae, the reader starts to wonder which of the two Roman commanders in fact won the engagement that day. Plutarch portrays Marius merrily charging off into a cloud of dust leaving those accomplished *littérateurs*, Catulus and Sulla, to bear 'the brunt of the fighting' (*Mar.* 26.3), which clearly implies that it was these two who dealt with the oncoming Cimbri in his alleged absence. Quite conceivably, at this juncture, Plutarch was again relying upon Sulla's *commentarii* as his source (*vide* Plut. *Mar.* 25.3). Still, R.J. Evans' rather bold statement that Plutarch's biography is so notable for its antipathy towards Marius that it 'ought not to be handled as if it were a historical account' (1994: p. 6) is perhaps going a little too far. Besides, as with many battles we look at, the truth often lies buried beneath many layers of retelling, in both oral and written history.

Two legionaries on the Altar of Domitius Ahenobarbus (Paris, musée du Louvre, inv. Ma 975). The battering power of the Roman army was provided by the legionary wielding *pilum* and *gladius*. It was neither *sarissae* nor bows, as in the Hellenistic East, nor slashing swords and spears, as in the barbarian West, but the tactical combination of *pilum* shower and close blade work that rendered the armies of late Republican Rome so deadly on the field of battle. For many recruits enlistment in the army was an attractive option, promising adequate food and shelter, a cash income, and a hope of something more both during their service and on their demobilization. (© Esther Carré)

AFTERMATH

Every hero becomes a bore at last.
Ralph Waldo Emerson, *Representative Men: Seven Lectures* (Boston, 1850)

POLITICAL WILDERNESS

There are two fundamental truths in war. First, the best war leaders are those who see war in the larger term, can look around corners, and can shut out the day-to-day noise. Second, incompetent, tired, and lazy war leaders quickly crash and burn. Marius clearly belonged to the first category. For that reason, Marius' consecutive second to fifth consulships (104–101 BC) can be seen as a popular measure, the people carrying a remarkable faith in Marius as the man they wanted in command, who should remain so until the Cimbri and Teutones were finished off. Naturally, Marius effectively exploited popular politics to achieve this unprecedented position because, constitutionally speaking, he should have had his command prorogued with proconsular status after his first consulship. However, in this situation Marius would have been handicapped owing to the fact that he could only remain in his command at the whim of the Senate. Worse still, in this time of crisis, the new consuls – for better or for worse – would have been his military superiors. As was glaringly illustrated by Caepio and Mallius, the working relationship between a *nobilis* proconsul and a *novus homo* consul could be one fraught with danger: the failure of Caepio to obey his superior Mallius and accordingly cooperate on the same battlefield had caused a crushing defeat and a lasting humiliation. As an elected consul, Marius was firmly in a position that gave him an unchallenged authority.

In retrospect, Marius' fifth consulship, which culminated in his victory at Vercellae and his triumph at Rome that followed, was the crowning point of his career. The afterglow of his *annus mirabilis* quickly established the notion that Marius was indispensable in the role of Rome's top war leader. According to Velleius Paterculus: 'His sixth consulship was given him as if in reward for his great achievement' (2.12.6). Others reckon excessive bribery was involved (Liv. *Per.* 69.3, Plut. *Mar.* 28.5 quoting Rutilius Rufus). Bribery or not, with six consulships and two triumphs under his belt, Marius had created an extraordinary precedent. At power's door, he was now a man above the Republican system, a forerunner of

Cnaeus Pompeius and Iulius Caesar. Nonetheless, at the time Marius' unconstitutional position did have a certain amount of logic to it as he was no revolutionary, and the existing political system in Rome had worked to his advantage. The other extraordinary side to all this was the temporary nature of Marius' influence.

There is an old Latin proverb *gladius cedet togae* (the sword gives way to the toga). If a man would be great, he must be great at home, too. After his defeat of the northern tribes, the serial campaigner Marius fitted the Roman image of the saviour-hero, and accordingly was hailed by the people as the third founder of Rome (Plut. *Mar.* 27.5), a worthy successor to Romulus himself and Furius Camillus – the old saviour from the war with Brennos the Gaul, the sacker of Rome. Unfortunately for Marius, it was not to be. The year 100 BC, the year of his sixth and penultimate consulship, saw the great general fail disastrously as a politician. In one of the many *volte-faces* of his political career, Marius would desert the tribune of the plebs who had previously aided him, the demagogue Lucius Appuleius Saturninus. Inconvenient truths are quickly discarded. In politics, a win is a win, or so Marius was led to believe.

The firebrand Saturninus had been re-elected as one of the peoples' tribunes for the coming year, but by proposing yet more radical bills, the Senate, who saw the spectre of tribunician government raise its ugly head as it had done twice before under the Gracchi, called on Marius to defend the state. The soldiers followed Marius' commands and defeated Saturninus and his supporters in a pitched battle in the Forum. Marius, having assured them that their lives would be spared, stood by as an angry mob stoned Saturninus and many others to death (Cic. *ad Brut.* 224, *Vir. ill.* 73.10). Having restored public order under the terms of a *senatus consultum ultimum*, both literally and efficaciously 'the ultimate decree of the Senate', the veteran general subsequently saw his popular support slip away. The 90s BC were to be a decade of political infighting of the extreme sort, and one of its first victims, according to Plutarch, was Marius. Yet his actions of 100 BC can be seen

Marius (?) celebrating his triumph over the northern tribes: silver *denarius* (Crawford 326/1) of the moneyer Caius Fundanius, minted in Rome 101 BC. The obverse depicts a helmeted Roma; the reverse a triumphator in *quadriga* holding sceptre and laurel branch with a youth riding the nearest horse. This triumph, his second, was to be the high point of Marius' extraordinary career. What followed was the lust for power and the fatal *hubris* that guides a man to his doom. (Classical Numismatic Group, Inc., http://www.cngcoins. com/WikimediaCommons/ CC-BY-SA-2.5)

Two legionaries and an *equites* on the Altar of Domitius Ahenobarbus (Paris, musée du Louvre, inv. Ma 975). The Legionaries wear iron mail-shirts, thigh-length with shoulder doubling for extra protection. The belt around the waist would transfer some of the shirt's weight (*c.* 9–15kg) from the shoulders to the hips. Each carries an Italic oval, semi-cylindrical body shield, conventionally known as the *scutum*. While the soldiers wear Etrusco-Corinthian helmets, the horseman sports a Boiotian helmet with a horsehair plume, popular with Graeco-Roman cavalry of the period as it provided unimpaired vision and hearing. The Boiotian was hammered out from one piece of sheet bronze, and can best be described as a bronze riding hat with a down-turned brim that has been bent into elaborate folds. (© Esther Carré)

as a bungling attempt to announce his arrival to the *nobilitas* of Rome. Of interest here are Sallust's remarks upon the monopoly of the *nobiles* on the consulship:

> For at that time, although citizens of low birth had access to other magistracies, the consulship was still reserved by custom for the *nobiles*, who contrived to pass it from one to another of their number. A *novus homo*, however distinguished he might be or however admirable his achievements, was invariably considered unworthy of that honour, almost as if he were unclean.

> Sall. *B Iug.* 63.4

Sallust takes leave of Marius at the moment when Rome looked to him for salvation (ibid. 114.4). The irony here is that, unluckily for Marius, to the *nobiles*, with their hidebound conservatism, he would always be, despite his unprecedented six consulships and two triumphs, an 'unclean' *novus homo*.

Despised by the inner elite and shunned by the equestrians and the people, Marius was now cast into the political wilderness. In early 98 BC, Marius did not stand, as was expected, for the censorship 'because he feared that he would be defeated' (Plut. *Mar.* 30.4). This was a clear sign that Marius was not in the political spotlight. In the same year, Metellus Numidicus was recalled from exile; Saturninus had orchestrated his banishment for Marius two years before when Metellus had stood against Marius for the consulship

of 100 BC (Liv. *Per.* 69.3–4, cf. Plut. *Mar.* 29.8). Marius, having tried to block the return of his one-time *patronus* (Liv. *Per.* 69.7, App *B civ.* 1.33), admitted defeat and scuttled off to Asia 'ostensibly to make sacrifices, which he promised to the Mother of the Gods, but really having another reason for his journey which people did not suspect' (Plut. *Mar.* 31.1). The undisclosed reason: stirring up a new war.

Marius had mastered the art of war. He was unrivalled when it came to wielding the sword abroad, but he was pitiable when it came to donning the toga at home. Marius wanted to beat the great families of the *nobilitas* at their own political game, substituting self-made support for their inherited connections. Showing little flair for politics, it did not occur to him – as it would to Sulla and Caesar – that the rules of the game could not be tinkered with. Though connected to the equestrian order by birth and interests, and favouring the welfare of soldiers – including Italians, whom he truly valued as necessary allies (App. *B civ.* 1.29) – he had no positive policies or solutions for the dire social problems of the day. Marius was not a natural demagogue, and his political future looked as fragile as his rise was spectacular.

As a man, Marius was superstitious and overwhelmingly ambitious, and, since he failed to force the *nobiles* to accept him, despite his splendid military successes, he suffered from an inferiority complex. The great general we military historians tend to lionize – visionary and victorious – is at odds with reality, for the pain of lost power was to bring forth a creed of a hideous hue. Marius the great general had a *doppelgänger*, a sullen figure mostly hidden from the public eye. This was resentful, disadvantaged Marius the failed politician. All this may help explain why, as his grip on power weakened, he disappeared down the rabbit hole of bitterness, bile, and defeatism – to which a younger Marius seems to have had remarkably little exposure – and later, vindictive cruelty: his fellow consul of 102 BC, Catulus, was among his many victims, which included some 14 notable senators, including six ex-consuls. Marius, formerly an upright, patriotic general, came to be viewed as an unscrupulous instigator of murder and civil strife. It is right to say that Marius' *doppelgänger* was a terrifying enemy of peace and stability, and as the luck of the civil war he instigated changed sides, he was to become the villain in his own narrative. This is Marius in his final form.

Yet the career of Marius marked a critical stage in the decline of the Republic, which would eventually lead it to its unhappy end. By creating a client army, which – with delicious irony – Sulla would teach his old commander how to use to good effect on the political battlefield as opposed to the conventional one, Marius was the first to show the possibilities of an alliance of a war leader with demagogues and a noble faction in the battle for power. Yet the uncomfortable, brutal bottom line is this: trapped between the obsolete and the utopian, his noble opponents, in their diehard attitude both to him and later Sulla, revealed their lack of political principles as well as their loss of power and cohesion. Sulla, a triumphant general of land-hungry veterans of his eastern wars, would apply the lessons of the preceding decades of factional warfare, and emerge victor and dictator. As per Hemingway's fitting description of insolvency, Republican politics goes bankrupt in two ways: gradually, and then all at once.

ABBREVIATIONS

AE	*L'Année Épigraphique* (Paris, 1888–)	
App.	Appianus	
	B civ	*Bellum civilia*
	Iber.	*Iberika*
	Kelt.	*Keltika*
	Illyr.	*Illyrike*
Ascon.	Asconius	
Caes.	Caesar	
	B Gall.	*Bellum Gallicum*
Cic.	Cicero	
	Att.	*Epistulae ad Atticus*
	ad Brut.	*Epistulae ad Brutum*
	Leg.	*Leges*
	Offic.	*De officiis*
	Orat.	*De oratore*
	Phil.	*Philippics*
	Prov. cons.	*De provinciis consularibus*
	Rep.	*De re publica*
	Tusc.	*Tusculanae disputationes*
CIL	T. Mommsen *et al.*, *Corpus Inscriptionum Latinarum* (Berlin, 1862–)	
Dio	Cassius Dio	
Fest.	Sextus Pompeius Festus *Glossaria Latina*	
Flor.	Annaeus Florus *Epitomae de Tito Livio*	
Fr.	French	
Frontin.	Frontinus *Strategemata*	
Gell.	Aulus Gellius *Noctes Atticae*	
Gk.	Greek	
ILS	H. Dessau, *Inscriptiones Latinae Selectae* (Berlin, 1892–1916)	
Just.	Justinus *Epitome* (of Cnaeus Pompeius Trogus)	
Liv.	Livy	
	Per.	*Periochae*
OGIS	W. Dittenberger, *Orientis Graeci Inscriptiones Selectae* (Leipzig, 1903)	
Oros.	Orosius, *Historiarum adversus paganos libri VII*	
Plin.	Pliny *Naturalis Historia*	
Plut.	Plutarch	
	Aem.	*Aemilius Paullus*
	Ant.	*Marcus Antonius*
	Caes.	*Caesar*
	Lucull.	*Lucullus*
	Mar.	*Caius Marius*
	Mor.	*Moralia*
	Sert.	*Sertorius*
	Sull.	*Sulla*
Polyb.	Polybios	
RG	*Res Gesta Divi Augusti*	
RRC	M.H. Crawford, *Roman Republican Coinage*, 2 vols. (Cambridge, 1974)	
Sall.	Sallust	
	B Iug.	*Bellum Iugurthinum*
	Hist.	*Historiae*
Strab.	Strabo *Geographia*	
Suet.	Suetonius	
	Iul.	*Iulius Caesar*
SIG[3]	W. Dittenberger, *Syllogê Inscriptionum Graecarum*[3] (Leipzig, 1915–24)	
Tac.	Tacitus	
	Ann.	*Annales*
	Germ.	*Germania*
	Hist.	*Historiae*
Val. Max.	Valerius Maximus	
Veg.	Vegetius *Epitoma rei militaris*	
Vell.	Velleius Paterculus *Historiae Romanae*	
Vir. ill.	Anon. *De viris illustribus*	
Xen.	Xenophon	
	Anab.	*Anabasis*

BIBLIOGRAPHY

Ardent du Picq, C. (trans. Col. J. Greely and Maj. R. Cotton, 1920; repr. 2006). *Battle Studies: Ancient and Modern*. Harrisburg, PA: US Army War College. 1903.

Badian, E. 'From the Gracchi to Sulla (1940–59)'. *Historia* 11/2: pp. 197–245. 1962.

Bell, M.J.V. 'Tactical reform in the Roman Republican army'. *Historia* 14: pp. 404–22. 1965.

Bishop, M.C. and Coulston, J.C.N. *Roman Military Equipment from the Punic Wars to the Fall of Rome*. London: Batsford. 1993.

Brunt, P.A. *Italian Manpower 225 BC–AD 14*. Oxford: Clarendon Press. 1971/2001.

Carney, T.F. 'Marius' choice of battlefield in the campaign of 101'. *Athenaeum* 36: pp. 229–37. 1958.

Carney, T.F. *A Biography of C. Marius*. Chicago, IL: Argonaut. 1962/1970.

Clark, J.H. *Triumph in Defeat: Military Loss and the Roman Republic*. Oxford: Oxford University Press. 2014.

Clark, J.H. and Turner, B. (eds.) *Brill's Companion to Military Defeat in Ancient Mediterranean Society*. Leiden: E.J. Brill. 2017.

Coarelli, F. «L'Ara di Domizio Enobarbo» e la cultura artistica in Roma nel II secolo a.C.' *Dialoghi di Archeologia* 2: pp. 302–68. 1968.

Connolly, P. 'The Roman fighting technique deduced from armour and weaponry', in V.A. Maxfield and M.J. Dobson (eds.), *Roman Frontier Studies 1989 (Proceedings of the Fifteenth International Congress of Roman Frontier Studies)*. Exeter: Exeter University Press, pp. 358–63. 1991.

Connolly, P. '*Pilum, gladius* and *pugio* in the late Republic'. *Journal of Roman Military Equipment Studies* 8: pp. 41–57. 1997.

Donnadieu, A. 'La campaigne de Marius dans la Gaule narbonnaise (104–102 av. J-C). La bataille d' Aix-en-Provence (*Aquae Sextiae*) et ses deux épisodes'. *REA* 56: pp. 281–96. 1954.

Evans, R.J. *Gaius Marius: A Political Biography*. Pretoria: University of South Africa Press. 1994.

Evans, R.J. 'Rome's Cimbric wars (114–101 BC) and their impact on the Iberian peninsula'. *Acta Classica* 48: pp. 37–56. 2005.

Evans, R.J. *Fields of Death: Retracing Ancient Battlefields*. Barnsley: Pen & Sword Military. 2013.

Feugère, M. (trans. D.G. Smith). *Weapons of the Romans*. Stroud: Tempus. 2002.

Fields, N. *Warlords of Republican Rome: Caesar versus Pompey*. Barnsley: Pen & Sword Military. 2008.

Fields, N. *Roman Republican Legionary 298–105 BC*. Oxford: Osprey Publishing (Warrior 162). 2012.

Forbes, R.J. *Studies in Ancient Technology*, vol. 8. Leiden: E.J. Brill. 1964.

Gabba, E. 'Le origini dell'esercito professionale in Roma: i proletari e la riforma di Mario'. *Athenaeum* 27: pp. 173–209. 1949.

Gabba, E. 'Ricerche sull'esercito professionale romano da Mario ad Augusto'. *Athenaeum* 29: pp. 171–272. 1951.

Gabba, E. *Republican Rome: The Army and the Allies*. Oxford: Clarendon Press. 1976.

Gruen, E.S. *The Last Generation of the Roman Republic*. Berkeley/Los Angeles, CA: University of California Press. 1974/1995.

Harmond, J. *L' armée et le soldat à Rome, de 107 à 50 avant notre ère*. Paris: Éditions A. et J. Picard et Cle. 1967.

Harris, W.V. *War and Imperialism in Republican Rome 327–70 BC*. Oxford: Clarendon Press. 1979/1986.

Hildinger, E. *Swords Against the Senate: The Rise of the Roman Army and the Fall of the Republic*. Cambridge, MA: Da Capo Press. 2002.

Hyden, M. *Gaius Marius: The Rise and Fall of Rome's Saviour*. Barnsley: Pen & Sword Military. 2017.

Junkelmann, M. *Die Legionen des Augustus: Der romische Soldat im archaologischen Experiment*. Mainz-am-Rhein: Philipp von Zabern. 1991.

Keaveney, A. *Sulla: The Last Republican*. London: Routledge. 2005 (2nd edn.).

Keppie, L.J.F. *The Making of the Roman Army: From Republic to Empire*. London: Routledge. 1984/1998.

Lewis, R.G. 'Catulus and the Cimbri, 102 BC'. *Hermes* 102: pp. 90–109. 1974.

Matthew, C.A. 'The battle of Vercellae and the alteration of the heavy javelin (*pilum*) by Marius – 101 BC'. *Antichthon* 44: pp. 50–67. 2010A.

Matthew, C.A. *On the Wings of Eagles. The Reforms of Gaius Marius and the Creation of Rome's First Professional Soldiers*. Newcastle upon Tyne: Cambridge Scholars Publishers. 2010B.

van Ooteghem, J. *Caius Marius*. Bruxelles: Académie Royale de Belgique (Mémoires tome 56). 1964.

Parker, H.M.D. *The Roman Legions*. Cambridge: Heffer & Sons. 1928/1958.

Patterson, J.R. 'Military organisation and social change in the later Roman Republic', in J.W. Rich and G. Shipley (eds.), *War and Society in the Roman World*. London: Routledge, pp. 92–112. 1993.

Randsborg, K. 'Into the Iron Age: A discourse on war and society', in J. Carmen and A. Harding (eds.), *Ancient Warfare: Archaeological Perspectives*. Stroud: Sutton Publishing, pp. 191–202. 1999.

Rich, J.W. 'The supposed manpower shortage of the later second century BC'. *Historia* 22: pp. 287–331. 1983.

Santangelo, F. *Marius*. London: Bloomsbury Academic (Ancients in Action). 2016.

Smith, R.E. *Service in the Post-Marian Army*. Manchester: Manchester University Press. 1958.

Spann, P.O. *Quintus Sertorius and the Legacy of Sulla*. Fayetteville, AR: University of Arkansas Press. 1987.

Syme, R. *The Roman Revolution*. Oxford: Clarendon Press. 1939/1956.

Syme, R. *Sallust*. Berkeley/Los Angeles, CA: University of California Press. 1964/2002.

Stilp, F. *Mariage et Suovetaurilia: Etude sur le Soi-disant 'Autel Ahenobarbus'*. Roma: Giorgio Bretschneider (RdA Supplementi 26). 2001.

Todd, M. *The Early Germans*. Oxford: Blackwell Publishing. 2004 (2nd edn.).

Zennari, J. *I Vercelli dei Celti nella Valle Padana e l invasione Cimbrica della Venezia*. Cremona: Athenaeum Cremonese (Annali della Biblioteca Governativa e Libreria Civica di Cremona, vol. IV, 1951, fasc. 3). 1956.

Zennari, J. *La battaglia dei Vercelli o dei Campi Raudii (101 a.C.)*. Cremona: Athenaeum Cremonese (Annali della Biblioteca Governativa e Libreria Civica di Cremona, vol. XI, fasc. 2). 1958.

Zhmodikov, A. 'Roman Republican heavy infantryman in battle (IV–II centuries BC)'. *Historia* 49: pp. 67–78. 2000.

INDEX

Figures in **bold** refer to illustrations.